Winning
Negotiation
Strategies
for
Bankers

Winning
Negotiation
Strategies
for
Bankers

Linda Richardson

DOW JONES-IRWIN   Homewood, Illinois   60430

This publication is designed to provide accurate and authoritative information in regard to the subject matter covered. It is sold with the understanding that the copyright holder is not engaged in rendering legal, accounting, or other professional service. If legal advice or other expert assistance is required, the services of a competent professional person should be sought.

From a Declaration of Principles jointly adopted by a Committee of the American Bar Association and a Committee of Publishers.

ISBN 0-87094-990-X

Library of Congress Catalog Card No. 87−70288

Printed in the United States of America

2 3 4 5 6 7 8 9 0 K 4 3 2 1 0 9 8 7

To Nicky

A financial sales negotiation takes place when the customer has one price or set of terms in mind, and you and your institution have another. Negotiating is reaching agreement on that difference in price/terms between what your customer needs and what you need.

Yes, you say. *I do that every day.* And you do. But how? Whether you are a commercial banker, investment banker, broker, or any other player in today's increasingly competitive financial services market, you cannot be sure of negotiating your next WIN–WIN deal unless you know *how* you did or did not achieve your last one.

With this book, you will be able to better prepare for the negotiation and actually *see* the negotiation process with a new awareness *while you are in it.* This awareness of the fundamentals and nuances, in turn, can help you *control* the negotiation process and ultimately *improve* negotiation results.

Many of you are already increasing profit and personal satisfaction *daily* by applying one or more of the techniques featured in this book. Indeed, this guide is based on practical, line-tested tactics of financial services professionals like you. If in reading these pages, you have a sense of *déjà vu*, this is as it should be— learning from your own intuition and experiences, reorganizing and refining what you know.

As with my previous books, I wish to thank my clients for sharing with me their negotiating concerns and their tactics, their questions and their answers, their

WINS and their LOSSES. Hopefully, this summation of their hard-earned lessons will help you not only get to the negotiating table but *stay* there until you can walk away with a WIN–WIN—with profit objectives met and client relationships safely intact.

Linda Richardson

CONTENTS

The Consultative Negotiation Approach: WIN−WIN

INTRODUCTION

Successful negotiation is a *skill* that can be *learned* and *refined*. While every negotiator enters a negotiation with the desire to have his or her proposal accepted as is, all good negotiators are ready for a process of give-and-take. A proposal cast in stone usually winds up as a monument to a dead deal. The winning negotiator knows how to use trade-off items to satisfy not only his or her own negotiating objectives but also those of the other party.

The objective of this book is to increase your ability to negotiate change in your proposal in such a way that both you and your customer come out winners.

Many people think that if there is a winner, there must be a loser. But in a really successful negotiation both parties can win. It is through the process of under-

standing needs and giving and taking to satisfy *needs* that WIN–WIN agreements are achieved.

At the heart of every financial sales negotiation is the fact that the customer has one price or term in mind and the banker/salesperson has another. These differences are usually quantifiable, such as prime versus prime + ½, or $12.00 an item versus $18.00, or a $250,000 fee versus $100,000, or a three-year versus ten-year term. The customer will often insist on his or her demand or "number" as a condition to do business. Successful negotiators are able to look at these *demands* as the tip of the iceberg. They know that the real threat or opportunity lies below the surface. They see their success not only in how well they can identify these underlying needs, but in how well they can present their institution's package and ideas so that the customer *feels* as though he or she has won.

One of the most successful ways for a negotiator to satisfy his or her own needs is to satisfy the needs of the other party. This is a simple but often overlooked truth. In an advertisement in the *New York Times* in 1985, Tiffany and Company showed its classic Tiffany diamond engagement ring above the title of the negotiation book, *Getting to Yes*. They were playing on the book's theme of giving to get: Giving the sparkler to get a "Yes." Similarly, a negotiator who can find out what the other party really wants/needs can use that information to reach a successful agreement.

The challenge, of course, is not to "give away the store" or "leave money on the table" in the process. By giving the other party what he or she needs, you are not precluded from achieving your own objectives. Unfortunately, too many negotiators think that if something is good for their own position, it must be bad for the other side, or that if it satisfies the other side, it must hurt them. Quite to the contrary, without mutual satisfaction of needs business would come to a screeching halt.

This book will not only examine the consultative style negotiation which aims for WIN—WIN, it will also look at the adversarial style, WIN—LOSE. Often even well-intentioned negotiators approach a negotiation with an adversarial mind-set because it is the only approach they know. But you can be different. Through consultative negotiation, you can avoid becoming adversarial yourself, and you can learn how to convert the *demands* of the adversarial negotiator or other consultative negotiators into needs your institution can satisfy.

This book will also help you learn the "secret language" of negotiation. "No" does not mean a flat "No." It means, "Not the way you put it just now." The challenge is to get around the "No." Negotiation is a language in which silence can be stronger than the most eloquent discourse, and in which, when a customer says, "X is offering us a much better package," he or she really means "Let's negotiate," not "Make a concession."

This book will also help you develop consultative *bargaining* skills because negotiating requires that you be willing to trade for value.

RELATIONSHIP BETWEEN SELLING AND NEGOTIATING

Negotiation is a process of strategies and tactics, not a result. Therefore, *how* you negotiate is as or more important than *what* you negotiate. During the negotiation each word has the potential to shift the scales and change the profits. What you do *before* you get to the negotiation table is as important as what you do *at* the table. And what you do before you get to the table is *sell*.

Unfortunately, many people do not recognize that selling and negotiation are a part of the same continuum. There is a mystique that surrounds negotiating. Negotiating is exciting. Negotiating is Henry Kissinger. Negotiating is a sharp executive trading off between the feasible and the optimal. Selling, on the other hand, is commonplace. Selling is door-to-door. Selling is Willy Loman. This kind of stereotypical thinking is part of the reason many people are not effective negotiators.

Selling and negotiating are interrelated. But you can be excellent in one yet very poor in the other. The best negotiators and salespeople are very good at both. While selling and negotiating are part of one continuum, they are *not* the same. If as an investment banker your stated price for an advisory service of $500,000 is accepted without discussion, you have made a sale, but you have not negotiated per se. It is not until your customer expresses his or her desire for better terms that the negotiation begins. Customers negotiate because they believe they can do better than would be possible without the negotiation. When your customer says, "My banker says he can do this for $280,000," the negotiation has begun. And that is when your knowledge of the customer, your ability to connect price and value, and your skill can make up for the difference.

The technical difference between selling and negotiating is that selling is the process of helping the customer decide to do business with you; negotiating is the process of working out the terms. An effective negotiator knows the difference between the two and does not make the fatal error of negotiating before the sale is made and needs are understood.

The "shifting period" between the selling phase and negotiating phase may last several minutes, several months, or longer, depending on the product, agreement, market, relationship, and complexity of the situation. The key is to know where you are so that you *do not negotiate too soon*. When the negotiating precedes the selling phase, the salesperson is usually put at a disadvantage.

Learning to make the shift starts with knowing where you are.

Negotiation is the part of the continuum in which the terms are worked out. The deal *shifts* from selling to negotiating as the *agreement (terms/price) begins to take shape*. As you move to negotiation from selling, the *intensity* of your transaction also shifts and increases.

The emotional intensity and tension that animates the negotiating table is usually absent in the selling phase. Most of this negotiation intensity stems from two factors: Each party has profit at stake and each party fears being taken or losing. Parties are not as tense in the selling stage because focus is broader and they are trying to determine how and if their institution's capabilities fit with the customer's needs—whether or not they and the other party can or even want to do business. As the negotiation begins, the focus gets sharper and the pressure builds. The issues being negotiated are very clear and the pressure to win not lose builds up on both sides. Because of this clear focus, and because profits are at stake, the situation can easily become explosive. Both parties can tense up and close up to protect themselves— and lose the deal.

One simple and effective way to defuse the intensity and defensiveness of negotiation is to use the selling phase to uncover information and build trust. Because the selling phase is not burdened with preconceived fears of winning and losing, it can be used to establish rapport and create an information base that can reduce and withstand the pressure. During the selling phase, information and even some concessions will be available to you that would be denied at the negotiation table itself when the pressure is high, colleagues are present, and the formal proposal is on the table. The negotiation is not the time to try to understand needs or build trust— by the time you are at that table, it is too late. The selling phase is the time to create the negotiation environment.

From the moment you sit down with a customer in a selling situation, say to yourself, "Down the road I may be negotiating with this customer. What happens now will establish the groundwork for later."

You should use this selling time as *lead time*, to get to know the product and nonproduct needs of the other party, to understand his or her decision-making process, to marshal support in your own institution, and to figure out your terms. You can use this time to plant the seeds for the negotiation. From the very first moment of your sales contact, you will set the pattern for how you and your customer will operate later in the negotiation. If, for example, you do *all* the giving during the selling phase, you will most likely continue to do so during the negotiation.

Sometimes you may not even be aware of where you are in the sales/negotiation continuum or even that you are in it. This can be very costly because you are laying the groundwork for what will follow. For example, an entrepreneur sent a copy of her new product to her former boss, the president of a very large company in the same industry. He wrote back to her to let her know how impressed he was with the product, enough to consider acquiring the entrepreneur's firm. The entrepreneur called him and said, "So you like my product." The president replied, "I like you. I want you to be happy." On the surface this comment showed personal concern for the entrepreneur. Actually, the president was *planting the seeds* and *setting the tone for the negotiation.* The negotiation in fact had begun, with the president trying to disarm the entrepreneur by suggesting it was her needs, not his, that were foremost in his mind. He positioned his interest in her product as a way to *help her.* His intent, however, was to put her off guard and keep the negotiation on a trusting, personal level. He later presented a proposal that was designed to meet *only* his needs (WIN—LOSE). Recognizing the negotiator as adversarial, even though he appeared friendly and concerned, saved the entrepreneur from a WIN—LOSE deal.

The following chapters will show you not only how to negotiate as a consultative negotiator (WIN—WIN), but will also help you recognize and control adversarial negotiators (WIN—LOSE) so that you don't get caught in WIN—LOSE agreements.

Negotiating Approaches

TWO APPROACHES

If you are a *consultative* negotiator, your aim in entering the negotiation is to conclude WIN−WIN agreements in which the needs of both parties are met. You also want to create an environment conducive for future deals with the other party. If you are an *adversarial* negotiator (WIN−LOSE), your aim is to take it all—to exploit the other side. If you prevail, the negotiation will end in WIN−LOSE and your victory will be at the expense of the other party. Consciously or unconsciously, you look on the deal/agreement/customer from a one-time perspective.

While these two approaches are extreme, they represent the two most common modes for negotiating.

Unfortunately, many *would-be* consultative negotiators are adversarial at the negotiating table because that is what they think negotiating is all about—"I win, you lose," or vice versa. WIN—LOSE fits the stereotypical image of the tough negotiator perpetuated by the media—adversarial negotiations make headlines that sell.

Many negotiators doubt if WIN—WIN is really possible at all. This stems from one definition of WIN: to be the victor—win the war. But Webster has another definition for win: to succeed at arriving at a state or place, and this does not limit winning to one side only.

If there had to be a winner and a loser in each negotiation, the WIN—LOSE approach would be justified. But more and more, WIN—LOSE negotiators are meeting with LOSE—LOSE results. Even in labor negotiations, long known for "toughness" on both sides, the adversarial style is being reexamined because of its costly and damaging long-term effects. The WIN—WIN approach is being recognized as a better and more profitable way to do business, short and long term, because long-term relationships are *built* on WIN—WINs. As effective negotiation strategies are analyzed, it has become apparent that the most skilled and successful negotiators are *firmly set on attaining their objectives, but they are just as set on helping the other party achieve its objectives. They know that is the best way to create the WIN for their own side.*

Given a choice between WIN—WIN and WIN—LOSE, most banking professionals would espouse WIN—WIN. They may even think that they are consultative in style. Yet only too often, in the heat of negotiation, they quickly resort to adversarial tactics. So it is worthwhile to learn how *not* to become adversarial.

A consistent consultative negotiation style pays off in many ways. Many bankers strive to differentiate their product/deal. The consultative mode of negotiation can help here. If you focus on mutual need satisfaction, your deal won't look like a commodity, because it won't be one. Secondly, the consultative style can help you control and often convince the adversarial negotiator because you stand firm while keeping communications going. Thirdly, WIN–WIN deals are less likely to get sabotaged and WIN–WIN negotiators are not dedicated to getting even. Finally, one of the most important advantages of WIN–WIN is that the world does not come to an end at the conclusion of the negotiation—WIN–WIN deals lead to long-term relationships and future profitable deals.

CONSULTATIVE NEGOTIATION (WIN–WIN)

The key to successful consultative negotiations is to *believe* that WIN–WIN negotiations are achievable and to *know how* to make them happen.

Without question, WIN–WIN agreements are the best kind. While you should do everything possible not to "leave money on the table," you should also do all you can to satisfy the other side and make sure he or she does not leave the table bitter and defeated, especially if you want to continue the business relationship or preserve your reputation.

WIN–WIN does not mean that you get everything; it does mean that you know and get your essentials. Being a WIN–WIN consultative negotiator does not mean you are easy on the issues. It does mean you are easy on the human beings at the table. Being a consultative negotiator takes *as much or more* skill as being an adversarial negotiator. Negotiating with a consultative negotiator is as challenging as negotiating with an adversarial negotiator because in all negotiations, *both parties are under pressure to get the best possible agreement* for their organizations. All good negotiators use their heads and expect the other side to do the same.

Being sharp and smart is not the same as being exploit-ative (adversarial). *Consultative negotiators always go for the best deal they can get, but they want the other side to walk away satisfied, too.*

The consultative approach will help you negotiate effectively with both consultative and adversarial nego-tiators. However, by using the consultative negotiation approach, rather than the adversarial, you will increase your chances for concluding WIN—WIN agreements since you will be better able to focus on needs, keep the lines of communication open, and work through problems.

Recognizing the Consultative Negotiator

You can recognize a consultative negotiator by the gen-eral absence of adversarial tactics such as threats ("I'll pull my account!"), ultimatums ("Take it or leave it"), or extreme/ridiculous demands ("2 percent put"). The following consultative cues will indicate to you that you are negotiating with WIN—WIN negotiators:

- They are willing to share information.
- They are willing to give time.
- They maintain open communications with you.
- They express needs up front.
- They ask you what you need.
- They give and take.
- They do not make ultimatums.
- Their proposals/demands usually have an ab-sence of unreasonable pressure or unreasonable deadlines.
- They say things that will keep the negotiation

moving forward like "Let's sit down and talk about this," or "Let's not get hung up on this point."
- They think about and come up with options.
- They offer a reasonable alternative or suggestion when they reject an idea.
- They are clear communicators.
- They use negotiating tactics, and expect and recognize tactics that you use, but they respond appropriately (bargain) when you test or challenge their tactics.

Understanding Needs

Being a consultative negotiator requires that you take the time to look at the situation from the other party's point of view. Consultative negotiators know that the fastest path to getting what they want is to find a way to also give the other party what he or she wants. This requires acknowledging what the other side *says* they *want* and then *finding out* what they *really need*. Much like the lines from the Rolling Stones' song, "You can't always get what you want . . . but if you try some time, you get what you need," an effective consultative negotiator knows the difference between "wants"—what the customer demands, and "needs"—what the other party wishes to attain via his or her demands. Consultative negotiators find out what is behind the want/demand because they know there are usually a host of ways to satisfy the need, but only one way to satisfy the demand. Once you know what the need is, it will be possible for you to find different ways to satisfy it.

A consultative negotiation deteriorates quickly into an adversarial negotiation when parties negotiate demands (usually fixed sums that each party says he or she wants). By working to satisfy needs, you can be creative in finding new solutions. Rather than digging in your heels about fixed sums (demands), you can be creative in coming up with different ways to get your "all-in" objectives met. This process of need satisfaction is achievable because few individuals have identical needs at the same time. By looking for creative ways to satisfy needs on all sides, you will work out mutually satisfying agreements that are better for the other side at a minimum cost to you. As a consultative negotiator you can aim at achieving the best deal possible for yourself while helping the other party to walk away winning too.

Reaching mutually acceptable agreements requires that you probe needs, trade, and find new items to bring into the negotiation so that the needs of both parties are met. The idea of WIN–WIN negotiating is not only ethical, it is practical. In today's highly competitive environment, customers not only have the sophistication to evaluate your proposal, they also have *alternatives*.

The key to being an effective consultative negotiator is to focus on satisfying needs: *what* you have to offer to satisfy those needs and *how* you offer it.

Although WIN–WIN makes sense and leads to better all-round deals, adversarial negotiators are all too prevalent. Therefore, it is essential that you as a consultative negotiator recognize the adversarial negotiator early so that you can avoid being his or her victim.

ADVERSARIAL NEGOTIATION (WIN–LOSE)

Hopefully, many of your negotiations will be consultative. Even so, it will be impossible to avoid adversarial negotiators. The adversarials want to *win everything.* They are the true believers in "All's fair in love and war and negotiation." Unfortunately, their victory would be at your expense. They view you as the enemy—to be defeated. In their world there can be only one winner and, therefore, there must be one loser. In the classic sense, they "go for the jugular." Their WIN–LOSE strategy applies pressure tactics to exploit you and get you to give in. They differ from consultative negotiators, not in that they drive a hard bargain and work to protect themselves, but in their objective, which is to *take it all.* In this they are relentless. Whether it is to use deceit or to make a concession they know you cannot accept, for them the end justifies the means.

The chief antiadversarial weapons are preparation, skill, and guts. If adversarials succeed in outnegotiating you, they feel you deserved your defeat, that "they did it to you before you did it to them." Interestingly enough, their WIN–LOSE negotiations are not always good for them since the LOSE side will, whenever possible, look for a way to get out of the agreement, sabotage it, or get even.

The best way to counter an adversarial negotiator is to (1) *recognize him or her,* and (2) be thoroughly prepared to use consultative negotiation skills.

Recognizing the Adversarial Negotiator

Here are some of the obvious signs of the adversarial negotiator. In direct contrast to the consultative negotiator, the adversarial negotiator:

- Claims to have no *decision-making authority.*

- *Makes extreme demands*—virtually impossible to meet.
- Takes and takes.
- Tries to get information while withholding it.
- Is in a great hurry, or conversely, has no time pressures; says things that will hasten the conclusion (WIN−LOSE or NO DEAL) of the transaction ("I need an answer on this by 5 o'clock today.").
- Makes threats.
- Says, "Take it or leave it."
- Acts overly dramatic or appears to be "a pillar of society."

Even if you find yourself negotiating with an adversarial negotiator, your *objective should be to reach a WIN−WIN agreement* and remain consultative. If WIN−WIN is not possible, you should WALK! Your negotiation motto should be WIN−WIN or WALK! Hostility, anger, defensiveness—becoming an adversarial yourself—will only thwart WIN−WIN results. It is often possible to totally control the adversarial by using consultative skills and countermeasures.

When you enter a negotiation that is clearly adversarial, you as a consultative negotiator should gear up for self-protection. Your "weapons," however, should not match those of the adversarial. Instead, use your preparation and your consultative countermeasures and tactics. If you adopt an adversarial mode early on, it will only further break down communications—you may intensify the problem, causing a deal that could have worked out to deadlock. Or you can become so emotionally involved that you push the deal toward a LOSE−LOSE conclusion. If absolutely necessary (if you don't care about the future), you can switch from consultative to adversarial at any time in the negotiation. However, in a business environment, while it may be necessary to WALK, you should do so without becoming adversarial and burning bridges. If you let ego get in the way in a negotiation, you may pay for it later.

The real disadvantage of switching to adversarial is that it is all but impossible to return to a consultative mode after trust has been destroyed. The Bendix attempt to take over Martin Marietta was a perfect example of this. By the time Bendix, the adversarial aggressor (we buy you, we WIN you LOSE) was ready to look for a 12th-hour consultative solution with Martin Marietta (how can we both come out of this with a WIN−WIN or draw?) the adversarial damage was done. In a reverse Pac-Man strategy, with Allied Corp. as its white knight, Martin Marietta avenged itself by buying the would-be buyer, Bendix. Despite the staggering debt both battle-weary companies had accumulated, the LOSE−LOSE marriage took place.

Other Outcomes

WIN−WIN and WIN−LOSE are not the only negotiation outcomes. Negotiations can also end as LOSE−LOSE or WALK (NO DEAL), or they can DEADLOCK. If you cannot reach a WIN−WIN agreement, which would be the next best outcome? If you are interested in profit margin, *long-term relationships*, continued business, and your reputation, the next best negotiation outcome after WIN−WIN is WALK (NO DEAL). Some negotiators are afraid to WALK and may be tempted to accept a LOSE in a WIN−LOSE in hopes of doing better next time. This is never a good move. Long-term relationships, business or personal, are built on WIN−WIN, not on WIN−

LOSE. WIN—LOSE or LOSE—LOSE agreements usually result in bitterness and dissatisfaction, creating enemies short and long term. The only possible exception to WIN—WIN or WALK is making a normally unwarranted concession in a particular deal because one party *has been* or *will be* compensated in another deal. Of course, for the "will be" to be defensible, such future business expectations *must be specified and committed to in writing.*

As a general policy, *do not accept a WIN—LOSE for a future promise.* If you let the other side negotiate the future with you, you will sacrifice your leverage and your actions will probably haunt you in future deals with this customer because he or she will expect more of the same. Simply put, when you accept a WIN—LOSE, you will have given up *too much* and it is very unlikely that this WIN—LOSE result will ever lead to a profitable long-term relationship.

The ultimate advantage of knowing the difference between WIN—WIN and WIN—LOSE is that you can avoid being trapped into a WIN—LOSE agreement and avoid falling victim. Once you sharpen your consultative negotiating skills you will be able to control adversaries and convert many potential WIN—LOSE deals to WIN—WINs.

Adversarial Approach

Adversarial negotiators deal through *manipulation.* They use a range of *pressure tactics* to defeat you and get what they want. If you are alert to their tactics, adversarial negotiators are transparent; that is, they are easy to spot if you know what to look for. Whether the pressure tactic is *silence*, which causes you to *drop your price without them uttering one word*, or *making a ridiculous offer* to get you to *lower your expectations* and your objectives, the aim is to coerce you into caving in. Once you *recognize* adversarial pressure tactics as such, the tactics lose their power.

Adversarials project tremendous, often unfounded, confidence. But with them it is the story of the *Emperor's New Clothes*. If you see what is really there, not what they want you to see, and act accordingly, you will not be fooled. But first you must *recognize* the adversarial tactics.

It is not a matter of tactics or no tactics. Consultative negotiators also use tactics, but they use them as a part of a *trading* process. You will be able to distinguish adversarial from consultative negotiators by *observing the key adversarial pressure tactics* that are listed in this chapter and by recognizing overall patterns and behaviors such as disproportionate or total lack of give-and-take.

Adversarials use pressure tactics *because they work*. But they work *only if you let them*. When you find yourself negotiating with someone you think is likely to be an adversarial, you should:

- Look for typical adversarial signals such as the extreme demand, no authority, no concessions, threats.
- Make sure you are *thoroughly* prepared, know your objective, and understand the elements of your proposal/terms.
- Respond only when you are prepared. Comment only when you are ready to comment, or ask for time.

- Test the other party *hard* by asking questions or remaining silent.
- Stay calm. Show confidence.
- Avoid taking things personally. Do not get overly defensive.
- Withhold details, especially in writing.
- Let the adversarial negotiator "win something" to save face but don't trade anything unless you get something back.
- Be persistent and maintain the inner desire to achieve. Work hard(er).
- Be willing to put in long hours of negotiation and to withstand a barrage of tactics.
- *Be prepared to walk away from the deal* if it is a WIN−LOSE with you on the LOSE side.

Customers will telegraph "adversarial" to you by their behavior and/or their words that they are adversarial. As soon as you get their message, you should gear up for self-protection without becoming an adversarial yourself. You can block them and even turn the situation around. You need not be victimized by adversarials: *You can deal with adversarial negotiators by testing them hard, being firm, and being confident.* You do not have to resort to adversarial tactics, and you do not have to offend the customer to protect yourself.

In the remainder of this chapter you will find key adversarial pressure tactics and ideas for countering each key pressure tactic. Following this chapter you will find in-depth information on the negotiation process, negotiation preparation and the consultative principles behind negotiation countermeasures.

KEY ADVERSARIAL PRESSURE TACTICS AND HOW TO COUNTER THEM

Ridiculous Offer (Extreme Position/Demand)

Pressure Tactic. Negotiators who make a ridiculous offer (extreme demand) in the early stages are informing you of their negotiating style. When they make a proposal that they and you know is totally unacceptable, they are identifying themselves just as clearly as if they were wearing a scarlet *A* (for adversarial) on their suits. If their demand is so out of line that it causes you to wonder if you heard the demand correctly, or if there is some misunderstanding, or if you are even talking about the same deal, you can be relatively certain that an adversarial has surfaced. The base + ½ customer who demands sub-prime, or the customer who refuses to pay *anything* for the ever-increasing cash management services you provide, is out for the jugular. The adversarial uses this tactic to *shake* your *confidence* in your proposal and *lower* your *expectations*. The tactic is designed to jolt your thinking and get you to lower the figure/terms you have in your head. Fortunately, the words of the other side do not have the power to do this *unless you let them.* Much like an orchestra leader, the adversarial signals to you to lower a "note," but you are not the first violinist and you can refuse to take the adversarial's lead.

If you recognize this tactic, you can take it for what it is, a tactic, and avert it.

Countermeasure. Faced with an adversarial tactic you must convey clear signals immediately. You should remain confident and not allow the tactic to influence your thinking or cause you to lower your expectation level or waver for a minute. You can remain consultative yet communicate a strength of position. One countermeasure would be to find out how the customer arrived at the figure or demand. For example, you could ask, "What is your thinking in feeling a 'drop dead fee' is not warranted for this transaction?" You could also use humor, suggesting he/she could not be serious. For example, an international banker confronted with a ridiculously low price demand once asked, "In what currency?"

If a humorous comment is not appropriate or if the offer is so ridiculous that for control purposes you don't want to honor it with a discussion, you can forgo asking how the customer arrived at it. Instead you could say, "Thank you for your offer. As you know I am interested in doing this deal but I'm afraid we are very far apart." Depending on how adversarial you think the other party is, you could add, "Since we are so far apart, I'd be interested in how you arrived at your figure." Again, however, if it is utterly outrageous, you can skip asking how he or she arrived at the terms/price and simply add, "Perhaps you can think about my proposal . . . , the value to you in that we . . . ,we can talk later. I can call you in a few days." If you want to play hardball you can add instead, "Think it over and call me." Another tactic you can use to counter the ridiculous demand is to remain dead silent; this should cause the customer to consider or defend his or her extreme position. If the customer is the next one to speak, he or she will probably back down.

Under no circumstances should you give any concession at this time. If your customer persists and you decide to trade a concession to get things moving, remember these points: (1) you must get something back for the concession, (2) the concession you make should be minuscule to communicate that you have not been swayed by the tactic, and (3) you can change the terms and reshape the deal to match the extreme demand. The key is not to become adversarial, not to storm out, and not to burn bridges. Simply recognize adversarial tactics for what they are and remain confident in the face of them. Test them and work to turn them around. If you cannot turn them around, be prepared to walk away from this WIN–LOSE situation.

Limited or No Authority

Pressure Tactic. Adversarials often claim they have no authority or limited authority. As soon as you find yourself negotiating with someone who does not have authority or has only limited authority, you should immediately retreat for the cover of not having authority yourself or find a way to get to the decision maker. If you allow yourself to be trapped into a situation like this, you will be the only one who can make concessions. This means you will give and the customer will take, or you will deadlock. Therefore, you should do something to prevent or correct this imbalance in authority immediately.

Countermeasure. Before you get to the negotiating phase, you should find out exactly who the decision makers and influencers are. Early on ask your contact, "After your approval, what are the next steps in the decision-making process?" If in spite of having done this, you find yourself negotiating with someone other than the decision maker, you have to devise a strategy to get to the decision maker. You must be careful not to offend your contact in the process. In many situations you will be able to get to the decision maker by focusing on a tough issue that only the decision maker can work on, such as personal guarantees or pricing. You can use the equal level tactic, of introducing a senior person from your organization, to enable you to get the decision makers to the table. You can also ask point blank, "If John can't be here, do you have his full authority?" and if the customer says, "No," you should postpone the negotiation.

Also, *whenever* the party with whom you are negotiating indicates to you that he or she must confer with X or Y for final approval, you should immediately introduce the idea that you, too, have X with whom you must confer. This will prevent you from being in a situation in which the other side has a fallback position ("the board said . . .") and you do not. (Please see page 40 for additional information on authority level.)

Few or No Concessions

Pressure Tactic. Adversarial negotiators want it all and, therefore, they will try to get concessions from you for free. Lacking a sense of fair play, they actually view any concessions that you make as a sign of weakness on your part. They will *demand* concessions, but they will resist giving anything in return. If you let them, they will take and take and take. They are very demanding in what they want but very sparse in what they are willing to give. When they finally make a concession, it will be small. They will have created an environment that has been so barren that you can be fooled into overestimating the value of the concession they make. What you must keep in mind is that although the concession has been so hard in coming, it does *not* increase its value to you. You can spot this tactic by the reluctance to trade concessions and the small size of the concessions. For example, if you are at 100 and the customer is at 40, the customer will begrudgingly move to 42. Adversarials will also make concessions that they absolutely know you cannot accept.

Countermeasure. Keep your total package in mind at all times and keep track of your concessions. When you make a concession, *trade it*—get something back. Do not be the one to make the first concession with an adversarial. When you do, make it contingent on getting something back and keep a running score. Don't make big jumps if the other side makes small ones. Use concessions as chips, one at a time. Be careful not to overrate the worth of a minor concession. For example, if the customer goes from 40 to 42, you should not retreat to 60 but rather 98 *after a considerable amount of time.* You should say, "Well, I really shouldn't do this but . . . , I can go to 98." And then be silent.

Avoid being the first to concede a major point, since adversarial negotiators do not have a reciprocal attitude. In all negotiation situations, adversarial or consultative, trade concessions slowly, one at a time, in decreasing increments. After you have made one *small* concession with an adversarial, get something back before you make the next one, which should be even *smaller.* If you proceed the other way around, smaller to larger concessions, your behavioral pattern will communicate that you have *more* room, causing the adversarial to simply go for more and more. When the adversarial finally wrings a concession from you, preface it with, "I really should not . . . ."

Keep track of your concessions and the concessions of the other side. Give nothing for nothing when negotiating with an adversarial, since he or she will interpret it as a weakness and go for more. Be patient. Do not panic and do not make big concessions right before the deadline.

Nibble

Pressure Tactic. The "nibble" is a tactic in which adversarials attempt to get concessions *one at a time* so that before you know it they have eaten all or most of the pie, bite by bite. They manipulate you by negotiating a point under discussion as if it were the only point of contention. For example, they may have four items they want to negotiate, such as fees, rate, tenure, and guarantees, but they get you to negotiate *each point* one at a time. You may make a concession on the commitment fee only to be told, "and we don't pay legal fees, either." With the victory over fees they move on to rate. They get you to make one concession after another without ever revealing the *full extent* of their shopping list—and you end up meeting all their demands.

Countermeasure. Your best countermeasure here is to get the *customer's full shopping list* before you make any concession. Don't guess at it—*ask for it!* You need the full shopping list so that you know when and how much to trade. You must keep *your* total package in mind, and you must find out the customer's total demands as well. When the party you are negotiating with says, for example, "The start-up time has to be moved up," your objective should be to stay neutral without committing. You could say, "I understand getting started is important. Let me make a *note* of this ... (write on your note pad). *What other concerns do you have?*" The customer may say, "Let's look at this part first." You can say, "Yes, certainly we will look at it. But to give you the best situation possible we need to consider the whole package. Let's see what we are talking about overall and then get to this. What other concerns do you have?" By returning to this question you can avoid costly mistakes.

Ignoring Deadlines

Pressure Tactic.   Time is a powerful factor in a negotiation. Adversarial negotiators will use it to pressure you into making premature commitments or unnecessary concessions. Adversarials count on you to take them at their word concerning a fire-and-brimstone deadline—and then ignore it themselves. They will say, "We must have the pricing by Tuesday morning," in the expectation that you will panic and cave in by Monday night. Then on Tuesday they will act as if it is any other day, leaving you wondering where the fire went. This is one of the adversarial's most insidious tactics, since it requires no overtly negative behavior on the part of its practitioner, who can always say, *after* you have made your concession, that the deadline has been postponed.

Countermeasure.   Expect adversarials to bluff about deadlines. Remember, every deadline is negotiable. Do not panic and give in as the deadline draws near or passes. You must be patient and wait it out. Patience is one essential quality of any negotiator. From the moment you enter the negotiation, ask questions about the deadline. Assume the *deadline is not real.* Test it. If a deadline is unreasonable, work things out so that you can deliver against it in stages. Remember, time is a critical factor, and if you don't have sufficient time you will make costly mistakes. Keep in mind the "Cinderella principle" so that you're not the one making major concessions at the 12th hour, when such giveaways usually occur.

Don't think that you have lost the deal just because the deadline has passed. In the legendary words of the baseball great, Yogi Berra, "It ain't over 'til it's over." Many agreements are reached *after* the deadline. You can also use deadlines to your advantage. For example, after *six months* of working on a deal, a banker said, "We need an answer in 24 hours or the deal is off." He meant it! Twenty-four hours *after* the 24-hour deadline the foreign syndicate came back and said "Yes" to all the bank's terms. Until they were pressed with a deadline from the bank, they stalled. After conceding, they said, "We didn't think you would pull the deal (WALK) and risk losing it yourself."

Deceit

Pressure Tactic. Some adversarial customers will point-blank lie to you or provide misleading or incomplete information to take advantage of you or prevent you from understanding what is really going on. The customer may say, "These are free and clear," without discussing a "minor" commitment. Or they will say, "Just do X now and I'll be fair with you," but after you do X they refuse to compensate you.

Countermeasure. It is your responsibility to test and double-check all information. Trusting someone is no excuse for not doing your homework, preparing and checking documentation, and monitoring the customer's situation on an ongoing basis. Ask questions and then more questions to find out what is going on. Get answers to your questions and do not assume a customer's silence means yes. You can be as badly hurt by a customer's omission as by commission. Under no circumstances should you give up your leverage by trying to negotiate *after* you have delivered the service or made the loan. Deceit is serious and you should discuss this with your manager and possibly your lawyer as soon as you discover it.

Threats

Pressure Tactic. Adversarial negotiators make threats to intimidate you and to get you to back off. Their aim is to create fear that the deal and/or relationship will be damaged or lost. They may threaten, "I'll pull my account. . . I'll move my business. . . I'll go over your head!"

Countermeasure. The key is to see the threat for what it is: a pressure tactic to get you to back down, not a literal intention. Your best bet in a situation like this is to acknowledge the customer's feeling and right to take a particular action. Avoid any hostility and then tactfully point out the benefits of not taking the action. For example, to the customer who says, "I'll speak with your president," you could say, "Certainly I understand your feelings about . . . and of course you can speak with . . . ; however, I want you to know I have presented your situation. In discussing this with him, we . . . , I have represented you . . . , *I know you and your account well,* and *continually represent your point of view.* Let's look at all the factors . . . ; I hope that we can work together." Assure the customer that *you have the support of your institution* on the particular point (make sure you do have it by doing your internal homework thoroughly) and present a unified front. At a particular point in a negotiation you must be prepared to call the customer's bluff, not by suggesting that it is a bluff, but by remaining dead *silent* or by saying "We want to do the deal but these are the terms." (Please see page 128 for Exit Close.)

Dramatic Language/Dramatic Behavior

Pressure Tactic. By expressing things in an overly dramatic fashion, adversarial negotiators attempt to put sufficient pressure on you to cause you to change your position. They may say for example, "This is a *disaster* for us. I can *never* trust you again. You are backing down on what you agreed to."

Countermeasure. Do not let extreme language influence your thinking or cause you to retreat from your position. Continue the discussion but do not budge. Realize that this is just a part of the process. Remind yourself that *a negotiation is an exchange of views.* Meet, talk, discuss, but do not cave in. Experience will help you become accustomed to this tactic and help you understand that while adversarial negotiators may make the moment look very bad, they often are willing to back down themselves.

These are some of the most common adversarial

pressure tactics. The first step in combatting them is to recognize them. Let's look at some of the many variations on these basic pressure tactics you are apt to face when dealing with an adversarial negotiator.

ADDITIONAL ADVERSARIAL TACTICS

Another Bank/Another Offer

Pressure Tactic.   Adversarial customers will often try to intimidate you by playing one bank against the other. They may simply say, "X bank has offered us a much more attractive package." Or they may give you partial details from the competitive package that is "superior" to yours. Sometimes they will fabricate a deal and refer to an *offer that does not exist* at all. More often than not, the information they give you is "cherry picking"—they relay to you only the most attractive elements of the deal, and they omit the rest—including the additional demands the competitor has made to warrant certain favorable terms. When a customer calls to say that another bank has offered a better deal, or an agent bank calls to say that no other bank has asked for so many restrictions (of course, he or she has called the other bankers with the same ploy), they are not simply stating facts—their objective is to pressure you to back down.

Countermeasure.   Whenever an adversarial customer refers to a competitive proposal that is superior to yours, it is important for you to show *confidence* in yourself and your proposal—confidence based on your understanding of your deal and the value you add. Under most circumstances, you should ask about the other offer so that you can compare them side by side. However, if you are confident that this is a ploy, or your price is in fact higher but your value is also higher, or you know the customer is very manipulative, you can refrain from asking about the competition, since asking about the competition immediately might add credence to the ploy and put you in a weaker position. The best thing to do in this situation is to *create competition for yourself* by indicating that you are confident in your package, and that you know, as does the market, the *value* of what you bring to the table. (To bolster your confidence, keep in mind that frequently your customers need you as much as or more than you need them or they wouldn't be speaking to you.)

For example, if you know that your rate/fee is higher but that your deal/product is worth more to the customer, you can create competition for yourself by saying, "Yes, we know X (competitor) is lower but of course I think you know we bring . . . . As you know we know your situation and the industry . . . , our expertise and our ability to meet your *unique* needs . . . , our office in Hong Kong . . . ." By pointing out the differences, demonstrating confidence in your added value and *referring to other deals*, you can create competition for yourself. *Confidence is contagious and persuasive;* if you believe in the value added by your institution, so will your customer.

Most often, however, it is imperative that you find out the specifics of the competitive offer so that you can compare *total* offers—apples and apples, not apples and oranges. You can say, "Since . . . let's look at the deals *side by side* (apples and apples) so that you can compare both offers." Or you can say, "Yes, I understand their fee is less than ours. May I ask the *other* terms so that we can compare total packages and values to you?" or ask,

"How experienced are they . . . in . . . ?" or "How long will they guarantee . . . ?"

Remember, no proposal or product is perfect. When a competitor is mentioned, do not become crestfallen. Ask questions so that you can *look beyond pricing* and compare the total package—pricing, terms, value, quality, expertise, customization, and so on—as a way to demonstrate your value to your customer.

Delaying the Decision/Starting Over

Pressure Tactic. Some adversarial customers look at each agreement as a starting point for the next round. They work a proposal over and over, making changes, negotiating every point to death, constantly delaying a final agreement. Every time you think you have an agreement, this customer will come to the next meeting as if the negotiation were just beginning. This tactic can throw you off guard and keep you going back to the bank for more concessions and more changes, instead of holding the line with the customer.

Countermeasure. First and foremost, have faith in your proposal. Always remember that your bank's package is *worth more* than the adversarial will admit. If you, yourself, come to believe that your customer is right, you will give in. Get the customer's *full* shopping list *before* making *one* concession. As when responding to other adversarial tactics, agree to do *X in exchange* for their doing *Y*. Especially when dealing with this kind of adversarial, *keep track* of all of your concessions. When dealing with the staller you should continue to reaffirm. If the customer wants to change a deal he or she has agreed to, say, for example, "John, we have already agreed to this. This is not a starting point for further negotiation." If the customer wants to "think the deal over" without making a commitment and you see signs of starting-over behavior, say, "Please realize that if you wish to change any of these points I have presented, then I would like you to know I reserve the right to change my offer to you." When all else fails, use the exit close. (Please see pages 128-31.)

Surprise

Pressure Tactic. A classic adversarial tactic is to introduce *new* information or bring up something "taken for granted" at the end of an arduous negotiation. The object of the surprise is to catch you unprepared and short of time to weaken your negotiating leverage. For example, everything has been agreed upon and the customer mentions something "taken for granted," or "given, of course," which is advantageous only to the customer.

Countermeasure. When the customer surprises you, you should see this as a danger signal and let the customer know it. Call for *time-out* based on the new information if you need it. Say that the new information is important and that you will have to look at how this affects the other terms already agreed on. Plant the seed that this may mean going back to the drawing board. Take the time to look at the information carefully, and do not make a commitment until you are fully prepared. Say, "I need more information about. . . , I have concerns about. . . . We would like time to look at it more carefully." One "small change" may have a substantial ripple affect on the rest of the agreement. It may also be the tip of the iceberg. To help prevent surprise, constantly check for new information or changes. As you begin each negotiation session make it a point to ask, "Has anything changed since our last meeting?" "Is there *anything* new . . .?" or "Is there any other information I should know before we continue?"

Emotions

Pressure Tactic. Some adversarial customers will use emotions as a ploy to embarrass or intimidate you. They may yell and scream, insult you, walk out, or cry. They do this to upset you. By getting you to feel embarrassed or guilty, they hope to get you to be easy on the issues.

Countermeasure. It is usually best to let such customers vent their feelings. While they do this, it is very important that you remain calm. Silence and a calm demeanor on your part can often help *soothe* the customer. If you can see through the psychodrama, you will be able to handle it. Even if you think the emotional reaction is genuine, it is important not to let it sway you or interfere with your ability to think rationally. You should show empathy, but do everything you can to get back to business. Your aim should be to be easy on the person but hard on the issue. For example, to the customer who is "hurt" and says, "I'm personally offended" by what is really a *reasonable, straightforward business request*, you could say, "Harry, I am very sorry you feel that way. That certainly is not my intention. Let's turn to . . . (the business item)."

Demanding Price Up Front/Ball Park

Pressure Tactic. When customers say, "Just tell me the price before anything else," they are trying to get you to negotiate too soon. If you give a price quotation before you know their needs, what benefits in the package correspond to their needs, and what your costs/profit are, you will put yourself at a tremendous disadvantage. Do not state price until you know needs and have discussed value. Avoid giving ball park figures. If you hand over control to a customer who high pressures you by saying, "Well, just give me a ball park. Your competitor was able to do so!" you will find yourself defending that price all the way down the line. Ranges are especially dangerous. Your customer will remember the lower end, regardless of what he or she says.

Countermeasure. Your strategy should be to *table* price until you are fully prepared and the groundwork has been laid. *Never* say, "No, it's too soon to talk price." Say, "*Yes!* So that I can sharpen my pencil, let me ask . . . ." And then you should get the *specifics*. The adversarial won't just ask once, he or she will push you again and again and you must be able to stand up to the pressure without creating a negative situation. You can do this by sticking to your guns. Say that in fairness to your customer you need more information or more time. When you do discuss price, you should be *specific* so that you can compare relative values. Some customers may not accept this and continue to press, "I just want the price." With hard-charging customers you must demonstrate conviction. *Repeat* your position. Say, "Yes, I can give you a figure very shortly, but I need to know . . . so I can give you. . . ."

Fait Accompli

Pressure Tactic. This after-the-fact tactic is directed at forcing you to accept what already has taken place. For example, the customer may file bankruptcy, then negotiate. One banker used this ploy with his own credit committee—he disbursed the funds before getting approval. He no longer works at that bank!

Countermeasure. Test this tactic carefully. Ask questions and get as many specifics as possible that you can use to plan a strategy of reversal or renegotiation.

Appearing Fair

Pressure Tactic. Adversarial negotiators will often say the right (consultative) things. But while their words work to seduce you, their actions speak more loudly and they belie their words. They may look like a pillar of society and say things like, "I want to be fair with you." Appearances can be deceiving. For example, in 1985 at a renowned private club, club members *trusted* what looked like "one of their own" and were taken for large sums of money.

Countermeasure. Apply the saying, "Thou shalt know them by their fruits" to adversarial's words. Look for fair *results* before assuming fair motives. Test and check everything. Do your homework. Trust *yourself*. Do not relinquish your trust to someone else. Avoid finding yourself lamenting, "But I trusted him!"

Uncomfortable Environment

Pressure Tactic. A customer may change the environment so that it works against you. He or she may arrange to have the negotiation at his or her office/home court to gain an advantage. By subtly sabotaging the negotiating scene (somber lighting, distant seating, and frequent interruptions), the "stage manager" customer attempts to throw you off by making you uncomfortable, hence, less effective. Second, any new or different environment (even an improved one) may cause you to be less assertive (studies show this, whether it is in a lab with mice or in a stadium with professional athletes).

Countermeasure. Don't be a victim! If you must meet on the customer's turf and the situation is uncomfortable, take the initiative to change it. Ask to have the blind lowered or your seat changed if you are uncomfortable. Avoid negotiating in a totally foreign environment. Combat the possibility of being less assured in a strange environment by visiting the site prior to the negotiation or by arriving early. Whenever possible, check out or inquire about the setting *before* the negotiation.

Also remember you can use the customer's site to your advantage because it can be *very revealing.* The CEO of a leading English software company was prepared to pay big dollars for a small Boston outfit *until* he visited their office. "We were prepared to pay top dollar until we saw him in his own space," said the CEO. "In London he was very comfortable and at ease. In his site it was apparent his company was not very developed and the product was not complete. He overly explained his cash flow problems and appeared generally uncomfortable."

"All We Have"

Pressure Tactic. Using "that's all we have," customers will try to minimize their resources to get you to back off from your demands.

Countermeasure. Test it. Get specifics. Use repetition and keep asking for what you need. Look for alternatives. If they only have X, explore alternatives for payment or ways to change the deal.

Lost Interest

Pressure Tactic. Customers may say, "Well, . . . doesn't sound as interesting as I thought it might. We'll have to give that some study and perhaps get back to you later." By acting disinterested, a customer may be trying to get you to sweeten the deal by pushing you back to the selling phase.

Countermeasure. Say confidently (without pausing), "I'm surprised to hear that. We are seeing tremendous interest especially in . . . market. What seems to have changed from your perspective?" Your objective should be to focus on needs, not terms, at that point.

One Party Leaves

Pressure Tactic. Sometimes a senior customer will walk out in a huff, leaving his or her junior associate or lawyer behind. The emotion-laden exit is used to upset and frighten you into thinking the deal is in danger of being lost. This could be either a "good guy, bad guy" tactic or a tactic designed to set it up so that you are the only one in the room with any authority to make concessions.

There is also a softer version of this game and it is even more dangerous and seductive. The decision maker will quietly and politely walk out saying, "Excuse me. I have to . . . . I'll leave you with John to wrap this up" or "I'll leave you two to work out the remaining few details." This is usually done to minimize the importance of concessions you are being set up to make. Those "few minor points to iron out" with an individual with no authority could be very expensive for you.

Countermeasure. When one or more of the parties you are negotiating with is about to walk out, consider this as a red flag and find out what it means relative to continuing the negotiation. *Before the decision maker leaves the room*, directly ask a question about the authority of the remaining person to carry the ball. You can say, "John, can I assume that Bill can continue this discussion with authority to . . .?" or "Bill, can you and I continue to . . .or . . .?" If Bill does not have negotiating authority ask the decision maker to stay or reschedule and adjourn. You do not want to be in the undesirable position of being the only one at the table who can make concessions/changes. Stay calm and mask any sign of panic when the dramatic exit occurs. Also, any time you observe an extreme good guy, bad guy tactic, you may say, "I'm sorry there is a dispute between you on this point. Would you like some time alone and we can resume our meeting when you are in agreement."

Outnumbering/"The Platoon"

Pressure Tactic. Some customers will try to overwhelm you with sheer numbers on their side. It is difficult to negotiate with a team when you are alone. It probably is not an accident if three customers appear when you were expecting one.

Countermeasure. There is safety in numbers. Ask "Who will be there?" and balance the odds by bringing along a team member to match. If more than one person is going to represent your side, prepare to negotiate as a team. When you are confronted with a team, be sure to clarify positions and roles. (Please see Team Negotiations, page 44.)

Paper Ploy

Pressure Tactic. Some adversarial negotiators will *prepare a document* in advance to enhance their position. The information may take you by surprise and is, of course, designed to work against your position. For example, one managing partner prepared for a salary negotiation by listing all of the partners' billings in order of magnitude. He presented this list to the partner who wanted an increase in his salary. Not surprisingly, when the partner read the list he saw that his name was last on it. Needless to say his negotiating position was weakened.

Countermeasure. Do not try to rush through new information at the point of negotiation, since your lack of time and preparation will put you at a disadvantage. You should say, "Thank you. I will read it when I can give it the time and attention it deserves." Then put the unopened document in your briefcase. In the above situation, the managing partner would have had to find a less elegant way to make his point.

If you do have to read information on the spot, remember *not to negotiate new information* unless you fully understand it and plan your approach. Ask for a break or reschedule the meeting if necessary. If the new information needs to be analyzed, say, "Let me give this the time it deserves. Let's get back together on . . . ."

Playing Dumb

Pressure Tactic. Some customers will play dumb to get you to lower your guard. They use the "Columbo tactic" of repeating over and over, "I don't understand" to frustrate you or wear you down.

Countermeasure. Be patient but firm. When the customer says, "I don't understand," *restate what the customer says* he or she does not understand—"I know you have said you can't understand why we cannot . . . ." By using the customer's exact words you show the customer that you have heard him or her. Then ask *questions* to get the customer talking and prevent yourself from becoming defensive. Narrow down exactly what it is the customer does not understand (place the onus on him or her to explain!) and then give your explanations one by one. By presenting one "argument" at a time you can increase your effectiveness. Don't give long explanations. Use repetition since repetition is an effective countermeasure. Avoid saying, "As I said," as you repeat yourself. Keep it brief.

Silence can also be an effective countermeasure. It requires that you have the patience and strength to keep quiet until the customer realizes the tactic won't work. If you can't keep quiet, you will leave money on the table.

Past Experience

Pressure Tactic.   Adversarial negotiators often refer to past deals or experiences to challenge your new terms. Their comments, such as "Last time we did this . . . ," or "John (your predecessor) didn't ask for . . . ," are really comparing apples (the past) with oranges (the present). They will use this rationale for getting particular terms that are *not warranted today* because of the changes in the market, in their own situation, or in your firm.

Countermeasure.   Prior to the negotiation, check into the relationship history. When you find it necessary to present terms that differ from previous agreements, make sure that as you present the new terms you *explain* your reasons and the *differences* between the deals. Explain the impact of a change in transaction size, the market, or the collateral. Customers need the explanation not only to be persuaded by understanding the deal, but also to be armed with reasons that they can present to their managers.

Silence

Pressure Tactic. During the negotiation, 30 seconds can seem like an eternity. *Without saying anything for a short period of time,* a customer can make a situation tense and uncomfortable for you if you are not able to withstand the pressure. For example, when you say that a fee of X is required, the customer can take control of the situation simply by remaining silent. The customer hopes you will become defensive, giving excuses and justifications and eventually talk yourself into making a concession. It is very important to return silence with silence. If not, you may find yourself caving in without the customer having had to say even one word.

Countermeasure. Patience and steely silence are called for here. It is important to resist the natural instinct to fill the void. As the salesperson it was your job to fill silences, but now as a negotiator you must use *silence to your advantage.* Unless you can do this you may find yourself lowering your price without your customer uttering one word.

Maintaining silence is critical after you have quoted price, since the first person to speak is usually the first to concede! If you must talk, ask a question rather than give an explanation.

Another version of the silence tactic occurs when customers do not return phone calls. You should be patient and plan a strategy for keeping the negotiation going without seeming overanxious.

Meals/Drinks

Pressure Tactic. Some customers will keep saying,

"Just 15 minutes more" at 7:00 P.M. when they really know that they intend to be there until 10:00 P.M. or later. Sometimes they will wait until the last hour to order sandwiches. They know you will not perform at your peak if you are hungry. In a restaurant, customers can instruct the waiter to take your order first, allowing you to order a drink before they order tomato juice.

Countermeasure. It's up to you to recognize when your energy and concentration are fading and to do something about it. If it is late at night you should reschedule or, if that is not possible, request a break. If you are hungry arrange to have some food sent in. Meals before the negotiation should be healthy and nonalcoholic to keep you sharp. This will also communicate seriousness and self-control.

"Take It or Leave It"

Pressure Tactic. This is an all-or-nothing approach in which terms are presented as final and inflexible.

Countermeasure. *Remember, everything is negotiable.* Say to the customer who demands ⅛, "I can hear that you feel firm on ⅛. How did you arrive at that? Think over my proposal . . . few days." Never say the words "take it or leave it" yourself since they are adversarial and difficult to retreat from.

"Don't You Trust Me?"

Pressure Tactic. Customers will say, "Don't you trust me?" to get you to shy away from a perfectly reasonable request.

Countermeasure. Be sure to tell the customer that *while you do trust him or her,* "Trust has nothing to do with it." One attorney says, "I trust you. If I were sure I'd be dealing with you in one year . . . . What if you or I were hit by a bus . . . ? We can all have that misfortune . . . therefore . . . is necessary for us to have . . . ."

Turning the Tables

Pressure Tactic. This is a pressure tactic that is used to get you to back down. You may be meeting with your customer to advise him or her of a fee/increase in what had been preferential pricing. The customer, sensing this is your purpose, will open the meeting by attacking present service or rate and demanding a *reduction!*

Countermeasure. Do your homework and know the level of service/satisfaction prior to initiating discussions of increased rate and fees. You should be prepared to *explain the differences* and the reasons for the increase. Show confidence in your new terms as you present your proposal.

Forestalling

Pressure Tactic. Some adversarials will say, "You're not going to ask for X!" even *before* you ask for it.

Countermeasure. *Be prepared to say, "Yes, I am"* immediately or your hesitancy will signal a lack of resolve on your part. Hesitation for even a few seconds will encourage your customer to push harder. Confidently and calmly say, "Yes, as a matter of fact, because of . . . we are looking at *X*" *before* the customer writes *X* off.

Time (Friday Afternoon, Appointments/Schedules, False Deadlines)

Pressure Tactic. Time can be used against you. For example, a banker could call you on a Friday afternoon to discuss a *small* point. By minimizing the importance of the call, "Just a few minutes . . .," and by blending in some social conversation, "I'm getting ready for a great weekend," he or she can catch you off guard and cause you to treat a serious point casually.

Schedules can also be used to get you to give in or relinquish your decision-making authority because of your schedule (you must catch a plane or train/go on vacation/go home/go to an event) and you cannot invest the time needed to protect your position. For example, one West Coast customer continually delayed starting the negotiation until 1:30 P.M. although it formally began at 10:30 A.M. The reason was that he knew his East Coast bankers had a 3:20 P.M. plane. These bankers invariably turned over their decision-making authority to the agent bank "to work it out." The agent, who was compensated for fees, was much more agreeable to lower rates.

False deadlines are another tactic that is used to put you at a disadvantage. Customers who say, "If you don't send it by 1:00, someone else will," are trying to force you to make concessions or premature/imprudent decisions.

Countermeasure. Be alert to the use of time as a powerful negotiating pressure tactic. Ask questions and *don't allow yourself to be pressured into a commitment* or *agreement* that is not to your advantage. In a negotiation, quick equals risk, and you should minimize unnecessary risk. You should not make decisions on the spot unless you are prepared to do so. Be prepared to reschedule or put in long hours, to change schedules, and to do whatever it takes to protect your position. *Invest time*—it's worth it! When you are exhausted, stop, since you will not think clearly.

Time is power, and when you need more time you should negotiate for it. All deadlines are negotiable. You should find out the reason for the deadline. Perhaps you can satisfy the time demand in stages. Keep talking, pointing out your value (you are worth the wait) to persuade the customer to change his or her deadline.

Wearing You Down

Pressure Tactic. Some customers use the five-hour nit-pick strategy in order to wear you down until you are an uneven match for a new negotiator. For example, a customer will labor over minor points until you are exhausted and call in his partner who is fresh when the major points are discussed.

Countermeasure. You should keep the total package in mind and pace yourself or you will be at a serious disadvantage. It is helpful to set an agenda of items to cover, to be aware of the time, and to move things along accordingly. If a new negotiator enters the picture when you are tired, call for a break.

"Let's Split It down the Middle"

Pressure Tactic. When parties begin to haggle, a very

popular pressure tactic is to get the other party to split the difference. For example, if you are at 100 and the customer is at 50, the compromise could be 75.

Countermeasure. It is very important *not* to agree to this early in the negotiation. The key is to convert the demand to a need by asking questions and then show your value (features and benefits) in satisfying the need. Your features and benefits will help you move your customer and you closer together. For example:

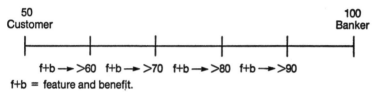

50
Customer

100
Banker

f+b ➝ >60   f+b ➝ >70   f+b ➝ >80   f+b ➝ >90
f+b = feature and benefit.

By presenting your features and benefits you can help your customer appreciate and pay for your value. When you do compromise, it should be toward the end of the negotiation, while avoiding the "Cinderella" concession mentioned earlier in this book. Then you can compromise between 90 and 100, rather than 50 and 100. If, after you have presented all features and benefits, the customer says, "Let's split the difference," (between 90 and 100), and you feel the concession would be too great, say, "That's just too close for us. The best we can do is 97."

SUMMARY

By recognizing such tactics you can avoid being the *victim* of an adversarial negotiator. It is important not to become adversarial yourself. By using consultative negotiating skills you can counter adversarial tactics and save your deal and your profit.

CHAPTER THREE

Four Negotiating Elements

NEGOTIATION FACTORS

Four basic elements determine how successful you are in a negotiation. These four factors are: power, time, information, and skill.

Power

Power is a state of mind. It is a multidimensional concept that involves how you think, feel, and act. If you *think* you have power and *project* it, you have it. If you don't, you don't. If you feel powerless, you cannot be an effective negotiator, because you are bound to communicate your lack of confidence. How you experience and express your power stems from the way you think about yourself. If you allow levels, titles, experience, age, and salary of the other side to dwarf your confidence, you will render yourself ineffective. When you *think* you are outranked, you *act* outranked. If you lack confidence in yourself, you probably endow your customer with more power than he or she actually has.

You can challenge a feeling of powerlessness by redefining the word *power* to mean "power to," not "power over." The best way to think about power is to define it as the "potential to *influence*, to get things done, and/or to control people, events, and self." If you approach your power as power to get something done, you are less likely to be awed by higher level, higher salary, higher position, more experience, or greying temples. These will intimidate you only if you let them.

The appreciation of "power to" can do much to equalize what could be an unequal situation. It could be intimidating for you if you are, for example, in your mid-20s, to negotiate with an experienced treasurer of a major company *unless* you are fully prepared and believe in yourself and *the value you (via your organization and your commitment and ability) can bring to the negotiation.* When you lack personal experience, you must leverage the experience of your institution. You can bring all of the resources of your institution to your customer's doorstep and you must convince the customer of this.

Your "power to" emanates from your *preparation, skill,* and *authority.* All of these are tied to your confidence. Your sense of confidence and power can be strengthened by:

- Your own knowledge and experience.
- The knowledge and experience of your institution.
- Your understanding of the customer's situation/needs.
- Your relationship with the customer.

- Your alternatives/flexibility.
- Competition for what you have.
- Your tolerance for risk taking.
- Your ability to walk away from the deal.
- The amount of time you have.
- Your institution's backup/standing behind you.
- Documentation (printed word)/or previous deals.
- Your decision-making authority.
- Your limited authority.
- You, yourself.

There are numerous sources of power but they are meaningless unless you recognize them and believe in yourself. Of course, which source of power to call on in a particular negotiation depends on the situation. For example, if a new competitor is trying to buy the business by giving predatory pricing (as a loss leader), you could call on your past relationship with the customer—". . . eight-year relationship . . . the acquisition coming up . . . ," your knowledge and experience to satisfy the customer's unique needs, and most important, your track record and consistency. Unless you draw on the total benefits to the customer of the past relationship, your customer may ignore the cost of the risk, what he or she may lose by changing institutions.

As for a level of authority, almost no one has unlimited authority. You may think that a *lack of authority* reduces your power. Quite the contrary, *limited authority* is a *source of power* during a negotiation. It is an invaluable tool for *limiting* and controlling your concessions and buying time when you need it. You can use your limited authority and still maintain your credibility, since *virtually no one has unlimited power.* Think about your authority level as your *influence level*—your ability to structure a deal, agreement, or terms so that they

are acceptable to the bank and the customer—a WIN−
WIN. With this attitude, your pricing/term authoriity is
basically limited only by your skill and your ability to
create and influence. One banker, now head of credit
quality in an excellent regional bank, says that he always looked upon his lending authority as equivalent to
that of his bank since it was his job to create deals he
could sell to both his committee and his customers.

As far as how to handle the full-authority versus
limited-authority issue, you should not *disclose your
level of authority* unless you are pressed to do so. Even
when a question is asked regarding your lending authority, you should not volunteer full disclosure of your
bank's decision-making hierarchy. While you should
always be truthful, since your credibility is more important than any deal, you should define your authority
level as your *influence* level. This level is based on your
ability to represent the customer in committee, to your
manager, or trader, or with a product group.

When Mr. Kissinger was negotiating in the Far East,
he said the *last* thing he wanted or needed was the "full
authority" given to him by President Nixon. "I was
horrified," he recalled. "I would be deprived of any
capacity to stall." Absolute authority stripped him of his
safety zone for limiting his concessions. Having limited
authority gives you safety valves and creates parameters
that you will need in the heat of the negotiation.

Whenever the other party mentions that he or she
has a higher level to confer with such as "the board,"
you should deliberately diminish your own authority
level by referring to your "committee," and so on. This
will help equalize levels of authority and help protect
you from being the only one with the authority to make
concessions.

Because power is a state of mind, you should make

sure that you do not allow your perception of yourself as the "seller" to work against you. If you automatically accept that sellers have less power than customers, you will weaken your own position. If you think the customer is all-powerful and you are at his/her mercy, you might as well not enter the negotiation. The extent to which this attitude can interfere with salespeoples' ability to negotiate has been observed over and over again in negotiation seminars when many bankers, who were *confident and assertive when they played the role of customer*, became less confident, less assertive, and less effective when they switched to the role of the banker. As the seller, you are not in a weaker negotiating position. The buyer would not be talking to you if you did not have something he or she wanted. By being prepared, remembering customer needs, and appreciating what you yourself bring to the table, you will keep your role in perspective.

Realistically assessing your customer's power can also help increase your confidence. You may think that your customer has more options than he or she actually has. When you evaluate your customer's strengths and weaknesses and consider such things as his or her need for the deal, you may find that you have an exaggerated view of the customer's power. Even though you are in a competitive environment, you should not assume that your customer has all the cards.

While you think of the strengths of your competitors, also think about their weaknesses. For example, one corporate customer was pursuing a very complex acquisition opportunity with tight time frames. He chose to work with his regional banker who understood the deal rather than shop the deal with larger money center banks. The key for the customer was that his regional banker had known about the deal for months before the acquisition took place and was fully prepared to act quickly. While the customer paid a slightly higher rate and agreed to tighter covenants, both parties in the deal got a WIN.

Remember that customers, too, can feel short on power. For example, customers in the middle market environment feel unimportant or powerless when dealing with a large institution. Impress upon such customers that you can use your ability and power to get things done in the most consultative and constructive way *for the customer*—to satisfy his or her needs. The quality of communication and depth of trust that has been built throughout the relationship will help you work with customers who might otherwise be secretive or difficult.

The first step in acquiring power is to know and believe that you *already* have it. True power is realizing that you and only you have absolute control over your thoughts, feelings, and actions. If you understand your objectives and needs and have done everything possible to work out the deal, you can WALK away from it if it is not a WIN for you. You lose power that is already yours if you think you "can't" when what you really mean is "won't."

Time

In a negotiation, time is power. Time in the negotiation situation consists of two distinct phases: (1) the lead time you have to *prepare* for the negotiation, and (2) the amount of time you have to complete a transaction. Each of these can work *for* you by giving you a comparative edge over your customers or *against* you by placing pressure on you. The party operating under the tightest time frame is at a disadvantage.

You should use *lead time*, the time before the formal negotiation begins (selling phase), as the time to gather information that will be more guarded or completely unavailable later on in the heat of negotiation. Lead time should be used to set the groundwork and build a positive foundation for the negotiation.

Lead time is the best time to develop information that you will need to achieve your objectives. You should use lead time to get closer to the decision makers and influencers, to gather historical information, to become more aware of both product and nonproduct needs, and to develop an information base that you need to negotiate effectively. (For more on using Lead Time, please see page 63.)

The amount of time you have to complete the transaction plays an important role in how well you will do. *Everyone has time deadlines. Regardless of how firmly they are stated, almost all deadlines are negotiable.* One bank acting as agent demanded a written commitment response from participating banks in 48 hours. The time was unreasonable, and when the banker probed about the agent's success in getting full commitments, he learned that the agent had less than half ($300 million of the $700 million). Of course, this deadline had to be extended. Therefore, don't be fooled into taking deadlines literally. Sometimes customers use *false deadlines* as a tactic to pressure you into making quick and imprudent decisions, or false delays to exhaust you. Customers can also take advantage of your own *self-imposed deadlines*, such as a time frame you have to meet, or a personal constraint that you allow to interfere (for example, a desire to get home on a Friday night)—all of which can lead to bad agreements or lost opportunities.

Acceptance time is another important timing concept. It is the *adjustment time* that one party needs to adapt to something that at first blush seems *totally* unacceptable. What one party may flatly reject at the first hour may sound more than acceptable at the 11th hour.

Time also has to do with *timing*. Timing is having a sense of when to do what. Timing is in many ways an art, but there are certain guidelines you can use to develop your sense of timing. For example, as previously mentioned, it is very helpful to *know that you should expect to get major concessions right before deadline*, not any earlier. Because of this, you should guard against the temptation to make a big concession before or at the deadline out of fear. Knowing this "Cinderella effect" will help you display the patience that is critical especially toward the end of the negotiation. *Patience* is rated by many noted negotiators as their most important characteristic. *Silence*, along with patience, is an important part of timing.

Another rule of thumb for timing is to *hold tough issues until later* in the negotiation, after a foundation of agreement and an investment of time have been made. For example, if a customer is adamant about no commitment fee, it would be better to present and negotiate other issues first. In most situations, you should not begin by discussing the commitment fee. The exception to this would be a customer who experience tells you needs a firm approach—"The commitment fee is not negotiable. We have plenty of other things we can . . . ." Good timing also means knowing when to bring third parties in, such as, "We don't think the lawyers need to be here yet. What do you think?"

Timing comes with experience. Timing means knowing when to focus on areas of agreement, when to tackle the toughest issues, when to absorb information, when to give, when and how to make a commitment, when to table an issue, when to take a break, when to call in third parties, when to change negotiations, when to throw out testers to get a reading from a customer, when to introduce an idea, when to keep talking, and when to be silent.

KEY TIMING POINTS

- Quick equals risk. The party working under the greatest time pressures negotiates at a disadvantage.
- Short time frames are most risky for the party with the least information.
- *Lead time* should be used to gather information that won't otherwise be available during the "formal" negotiation.
- Most *deadlines* are *negotiable.*
- Customers use false deadlines to pressure you.
- Negotiators can become their own enemies by placing time pressures on themselves.
- Toughest issues should be negotiated later, after time and energy are invested and trust is established.
- The most important customer concessions will come at the last possible hour. Don't panic and make your big concession then.
- *Acceptance time* is an important timing concept; today's "No" is tomorrow's "Yes."

Information

The third major negotiation element is information. Information equates to relationship. Information is money. *Information is power*. Lack of information can render you vulnerable and therefore you should develop as much information as possible. You must test every assumption, leave no stone unturned, and get to know your customer. You should ask questions (for example, why a particular deadline is set when it is), do analyses, study files, consider your past negotiation experience with the customer, test *all* assumptions, check and recheck your data, and determine what is at stake for all parties.

Some adversarial negotiators may deliberately deceive you, and unless you test and check out the information they give you, you will become their victim. Since they often appear to be fair, you must *force* yourself to test and check. This theme, the perils of trusting "one of your own kind," is central in the spy novels by John Le Carré. MI6 (British Intelligence) cannot believe that a member of "The Old Boys' Club" could possibly be a KGB agent (Russian Intelligence), and so cannot see the obvious deception in front of their eyes.

The information you develop should include a full analysis of the customer, his or her needs, decision-making process, alternatives, options, time frames, limits, and appetite for risk. This will help improve your negotiation position and reduce surprises.

Skill

Time, power, and information are interrelated elements—information is power and time is power. Your skill level will determine how you use these elements to your advantage. How skillful you are at the negotiating table is a key factor in how you fare in the negotiation. Skill is the *how*. Many negotiators feel the how is *more* important than the *what* (the actual deal). The following chapters will take an in-depth look at the process of negotiating and at specific tactics you can use at the negotiating table to protect your profits and satisfy the needs of the other side at the same time.

CHAPTER FOUR

Preparation for a Consultative Negotiation

PLANNING FOR THE NEGOTIATION

One of the best ways to avoid a bad deal is to prepare. Preparation will enable you to build a foundation in which power, time, information, and skill can work for you.

BEFORE GOING TO THE BARGAINING TABLE

Using Lead Time

When the formal negotiation begins, when proposals are put on the table, the *fears* associated with the traditional WIN−LOSE negotiation emerge and parties become defensive. Customers who are open during the lead time of the selling phase are often much less willing to divulge information or make concessions at the negotiating table. Even in the best negotiation situations—ones in which there is trust—parties are more guarded.

Therefore, lead time (not later!) is the time to:

- Build a foundation of trust that can sustain the heat of the negotiation.
- Define the issues and potential barriers.
- Identify and understand what the customer needs and what you need.
- Gather facts and data to control the negotiation, reduce pressure, and open what otherwise would have been a "closed book" during the negotiation.
- Establish a pattern of trading on the part of both parties.
- Marshal support within the company (develop relationships with influencers and decision makers in the company).
- Develop the customer's investment in wanting to do the deal.
- Determine what is at stake.
- Strive for an equilibrium (not being too easy or too hard).
- Establish the relationship and two-way communication pattern that will be carried into the negotiation phase.
- Set realistic expectations (plant the seed).
- Develop your negotiation objectives.
- Develop your *proposal*:
  - Prepare information and materials needed to open the negotiation.
  - Determine opening figures.
  - Build *flexibility* into your proposal (if the negotiation cannot bend, it will break!).

- Develop alternatives (think "what if ... "); consider options you might bring into the negotiation.
- Analyze your customer's strengths and weaknesses.

During lead time it is often advantageous to meet with customers and influencers (both inside and outside the company) such as lawyers, accountants, and so on, so that you can ensure that all interests are considered, product and nonproduct (emotional) needs are uncovered, and support is marshaled prior to developing and presenting your proposal. You can use one-on-one meetings to check attitudes, identify needs, and prepare for the negotiation, saving many hours and dollars. One of the most serious errors you can make is to develop a proposal that does not expressly address the *customer's needs.*

Customer Use of Lead Time

The value of lead time is appreciated by most customers. Therefore, you should be careful about what you say "off the record," what you commit to, what concessions you make, and what information you disclose during lead time. Since your customer knows the value of lead time, this is the time to begin the pattern of trading and giving only if you get!

Proposals

Proposals should contain more than the terms of the deal. One of the major flaws in most financial sales proposals is that they do not include customer *needs* and they do not contain flexible elements that add up to an all-in objective. Proposals that sell are proposals that satisfy needs and give the negotiator the flexibility needed to change as the deal takes shape. Preplanned trade-offs/concessions and options are needed during the bargaining phase and they must be planned for as you develop your proposal.

Sometimes it is necessary to send a proposal prior to the meeting. This can be a problem, as it generates unnecessary work ("Send me a proposal" can be a customer smoke screen), limits the flexibility that is possible with a personal presentation, and gives the customers a document to use to shop the deal. Charging a customer an up-front fee for the proposal can often deter this, especially when the deal is large enough. It is usually much better for you to be there when your customer receives your proposal.

If you are obliged to send a proposal in advance, it is *very* important to make sure that as you do so you *begin the trading process*, that is, that you *get something from the customer in exchange for sending the proposal. A fair exchange* from the customer for developing a proposal would be *information* on the situation, needs, and requirements. You can say, "So that I can address your needs more specifically, I'd like to ask some additional questions. Can you tell me . . . ?" Not only will this establish the trading process and set the pattern for "down the road," but more importantly, it will give you a way to differentiate your proposal by addressing *specific customer needs*. Customers who refuse to give information may be signaling to you that they are adversarial or that they are shopping the deal. You should develop the key elements of your proposal *with* your customer. Unless you identify needs prior to sending a proposal, you will have little chance of differentiating your proposal from your competitor's—unless your competitor has taken a consultative approach, in which case your proposal will be inferior! In today's competitive market it is very difficult to win a good deal with a needs-blind proposal.

When you are requested to send your proposal in advance, arrange a follow-up meeting to get face-to-face feedback on the proposal after the customer has received it.

Internal Credibility

To develop truly WIN–WIN proposals, you must network within your organization so that your proposals are accepted in the first place and supported down the line. Your internal credibility is a major factor in how much flexibility you will be given to negotiate with your customers. Your internal credibility stems from your reputation, *personal credibility*, and tenure, as well as how prepared you are with facts and figures, especially pricing. You should be prepared to present a detailed analysis of your customer's business situation and an understanding of his or her business, not just the mechanics and numbers. Be prepared to summarize and to answer questions such as: "What do you see as the risks?" "Do you know the management?" "What's the company's track record?" And for credit situations, you should also be prepared to give assurances of repayment.

Discuss your strategy with your managers and marshal their support *before* you make your internal presentation. By involving managers, product specialists, pricing committee members, and lawyers early in the process, you can develop the internal support you will need for approval. By knowing where the bank stands, you can avoid raising unrealistic expectations in your customer's mind as the deal or agreement develops.

Some guidelines for negotiating internally:

- Presell and line up support before the meeting.
- Be fully prepared. People are busy. Have facts and figures lined up that will satisfy the concerns and needs of the deciders. Present them clearly and quickly.
- Know the product and nonproduct needs of the deciders. For example, a product need for the senior manager approving the deal may be to get a yield of X for risk protection but the noncredit need may be ego satisfaction ("They now do large blocks with X firm.") or to be perceived as innovative.
- Be confident and show conviction.
- Identify assumptions as such.
- When you don't know an answer or you are not prepared to answer, say "I don't know, I'll find out"—*your credibility is at stake!*
- Know policy guidelines and other criteria—and if you are seeking something that is *against* policy you should be the one to point this out.
- Know your objectives (your all-in desired results).
- Ask for assistance if you need it. Develop personal internal relationships by building a network and supporters who will be there when you need them.

Your goal in internal negotiations, like negotiations with the customer, is to achieve your objectives. Therefore you should have a clear idea of those objectives prior to your internal meetings. Your aim should be to get parameters so that you have flexibility when you meet with the customer. Think about your objective in terms of yield so that you can vary the elements that comprise the price. Getting a range will give you flexibility; however, your committee, trader, or manager must be convinced that you will not automatically go for the lower end. Having the flexibility will enable you to convey a needed level of authority to the customer.

If you really believe in your proposal, you should not go so far as to put your job on the line, but you should put a lot on the line. By demonstrating preparation and your team's commitment you should make it hurt more for your committee or manager to say "No" than to say "Yes." One banker, highly professional and very talented, upon learning that a creative financing package he devised for a fast food franchise specializing in chicken was dead, presented his senior manager with a box containing chicken bones! He may have been walking on eggshells but he got the approval he sought!

Keep in mind that you are not the only one who has to negotiate internally. Everyone has behind-the-scenes decision makers and influencers, and all parties are under pressure from both sides.

PREPARING FOR THE NEGOTIATION WITH YOUR CUSTOMER

When negotiators are asked why bad deals are made, they usually attribute the bad deal to a lack of preparation. To avoid WIN–LOSE deals and to maximize the opportunity for WIN–WIN agreements, it is *essential* that you prepare thoroughly for the negotiation. You can count on one thing: Negotiations with adversarial or consultative negotiators will be rigorous.

The following specific information should be fully organized prior to sitting down at the negotiation table:

Set Your Objective for Final Agreement

One of the most important tasks as you prepare is to set an *output objective*. This is what you want to walk away with. Your objective should be viewed as the *total yield*, rather than as a fixed demand, since there are probably several different combinations that can add up to achieving it. Your objective should be visible to you because if you can see it you are more likely to go after and get it. It should be quantifiable and measurable. You can test your objective (X) to make sure it is an output objective by asking yourself, "What will I *see* to tell me that I achieved X?" For example, you may initially think that your objective is to "Get the best possible deal." This "fuzzy" (subjective) objective is worthless in the heat of a negotiation because it doesn't help you hold the line as you shape the agreement. By asking yourself the question, "What will I see at the conclusion of the negotiation that would tell me it is the best possible deal?" you could transform this fuzzy objective into a measurable one. Measurable criteria could be 80 point spread, or 1½ points over parent's rate, collateral of Y, $8 per item, or $130,000 fee—all criteria that can be measured objectively. *Either you get it or you don't.*

Having an output objective enables you to keep track of *where* you are in the deal and to evaluate what you have achieved when the negotiation is over. By quantifying your *expectation* level you can help make sure that what you are asking for is *high* enough while at the same time attainable. Having a clear target helps you withstand pressure, especially with adversarials. In a negotiation you must know what is important to you and then focus on getting it. By knowing your parameters, you can avoid bad deals—deals in which you would not be adequately compensated.

Your output objective should be as high as your *expectation* objective. As you set it, *aim high.* Your expectation level will affect your outcome. Ask for what you are worth and do not underestimate yourself. Once you set your output objective, you must make decisions about your *opening terms* and *bottom line.*

Decide on Opening Figures

Deciding opening figures takes knowledge and experience. How you open is important because it sets the tone for the negotiation, establishes the level of expectation for the *outcome.* It gives you room to negotiate. How your customer opens will give you an indication of his or her negotiation style; extreme opening demands signal an adversarial.

You should guard against opening with terms that are too low or you will leave money on the table simply because you *do not* ask for enough up front. If you set your objective and ask for it, there is *more* of a chance that you will get it than if you don't ask for it. One banker asked for $100,000 in fees for a particular deal. When discussing the deal after it closed, she said, "I looked the customer in the eye and asked for it, because I knew we were worth it. I thought my colleague was going to faint when the customer agreed without any discussion. I was prepared and determined because I knew we were worth it!"

Of course, you should exercise judgment in choosing your opening figures. As you set your opening terms, take into account your customer and his or her negotiation style. If you need more negotiating room, open *higher.* If you need room, be sure to build adequate flexibility into your opening terms, and develop a plan for how and what you will trade once the bargaining begins. Consider your customer, your market, and your competition to determine how much and what kind of negotiating room you will need. Sometimes you must sharpen your pencil, particularly in a competitive market or bidding-type situation in which greedy negotiators do not get a second chance. You may feel, because of your customer or market, that you should come in "right on the nose" in the rate/fee. Even so, you *must* leave some negotiating room elsewhere, or your negotiation will not be a negotiation, it will be an offer. Too often bankers come in on the nose when the situation clearly would allow for room based on the relationship, particular negotiating style of the customer, lack of competition, time pressures the customer is facing, bank expertise, and so on. In deciding how much negotiating room you need, evaluate each situation and use your judgment. When you do build in negotiating room, be prepared to justify your terms and to justify your concessions. A rule of thumb to maintain credibility is, "Change the price (terms),change the deal." Ask yourself, "What can I take out or put in?" The more flexibility and options you have, the easier it will be to negotiate successfully.

Give thought to your opening terms vis-à-vis your aspiration level. Be prepared to nondefensively explain the reason for the terms as you present them. Don't open with your best offer if you will need room and flexibility. *Opening terms* are frequently viewed as a *starting point*; therefore, you should give yourself the amount of room that *analysis*, *experience*, and the *competitive environment* say you will need. You must believe in what you ask for, if your customer is to accept it.

Identify Needs

Needs are the cornerstone of consultative negotiations. Identification and satisfaction of needs make WIN—WIN possible. Understanding needs will allow you to shift ground from demands to an area in which alternatives and flexibility are possible. Therefore, it is important to keep needs paramount in your mind before as well as during the negotiation. There is a natural inclination among negotiators to focus on demands. Demands are not the same as needs, although *needs may be expressed as demands.* Demands are fixed sums ($8.00 an item or LIBOR + 1) or a fixed position (no guarantees). Negotiating demands can cause you to lock horns, since customer demands and bank demands are frequently at odds. Needs are the underlying motivation behind a particular demand. Meeting the demand itself is only one solution among many. By identifying needs before you negotiate, you will be able to see paths and ways to give the other side what he or she needs and also get what you need. Your aim should be to find out *what the customer's needs are*—that is, to find out what he or she wishes to achieve. Identify product and nonproduct needs of all the decision makers and influencers so that you can develop your proposal with optimum chances for acceptance.

Keep in mind the two basic kinds of needs— product and nonproduct (emotional). Product needs are very important. These are related to the business and are in sync with the company's way of doing business— risk-averse, cash flow, and so on. The individual you are negotiating with fits into his or her company's business culture and, therefore, the customer's style of doing business will match that of his company.

Nonproduct needs are more difficult to assess. Nonproduct needs are related to the individual him- or herself. One successful negotiator says that to gain insight into what makes his customers tick, he finds out how they get their bonuses. Satisfying emotional needs—confidence, pride, ego, trust, dealing with someone they like, getting VIP treatment—can make the difference between a deal that falls apart and one that closes. If you know what the *other party needs*, you can deliver it to get what *you need!*

Often *needs of either kind are not expressed at all.* Customers don't say, "I want prime because my ego needs it," or, "I want to pay no more than $200,000 because I want to look good," or "I don't trust you and I am pushing/testing you to make sure . . . ." Demands, the tip of the iceberg, are what are presented to you. Needs are really what it is all about, and therefore, you should take the time to identify the needs below the surface. The best time to really understand needs is *before* you get to the bargaining table. This is when parties are more open and less defensive.

The difference between demands and needs is more than semantics. There are numerous ways to satisfy a need, but there is only one way to meet a demand and that is with the demand itself. For example, one party will say ½ and the other party will say 1. These demands are in conflict but needs may not be in conflict. Actually *few people have identical needs* at the same time. Rather than arguing demands such as 85 versus 95 basis points, or X in fees versus Y in fees, or guarantees versus no guarantees, you should ask "Why?" to uncover the need behind the demand. By understanding why a customer demands ½, you can often identify needs that can be met in several ways and creatively explore options. You can use your trade-off items or you can identify aspects of the deal that you might not have considered.

Looking beyond the demand will also help you control customers who use false demands as pressure tactics. Asking "Why" will help you stand firm and force the customer to back up his or her demand.

Interestingly enough, meeting a demand will not necessarily satisfy the customer. Satisfaction is partly rational and partly emotional. A customer who says, "It's not our policy to pay legal fees" will probably be less satisfied with a knee-jerk 100 percent waiver of the legal fee than the customer who works hard to get a 20 percent reduction based on a thorough fee analysis that calculates the hours involved, itemizes legal work, and brings to light the unique circumstances and time pressures involved in closing the deal! A customer can get a great price and *not be satisfied*. Regardless of how good the price is objectively, if it comes too easily, customers will feel dissatisfied because it will cause them to *think* they could have done better. The point is that satisfying demands—even price demands—will not necessarily satisfy the customer.

Understanding needs, yours and your customer's, is the most important task you can accomplish. It will enable you to be creative in developing ideas and options to help you satisfy them.

Develop Your Strategy

If you don't have the *right* strategy, you may find that regardless of how good your deal is and how excellent your skills are or how much time you have, you may never successfully close a deal. Your strategy is really your *grand plan* for *achieving your objectives*. To help you think about your strategy, you can use a four-point checklist: people, place, time, benefits. When all of these are present, you have an excellent opportunity for success.

People

- Planning with whom to negotiate—the subsidiary or parent principle, or both?
- Arranging for your managing partner to call the CFO.
- Identifying key economic decision makers and influencers.
- Getting the *right* people at the negotiating table.
- Covering your bases with influencers beforehand.
- Negotiating as a team or negotiating alone.
- Assigning one team member to keep track of concessions.
- Balancing the numbers (for example, matching the three negotiators from the other side with three negotiators from your side).

Place

- Negotiating at your site/their site.
- Setting up integrated seating (not "us against them").

Time

- Taking advantage of a "window" in the market.
- Deciding whether to send your proposal in advance.
- Determining the order of points you will *negotiate* first.

- Determining the order of trade-off items you will *trade* first and what to open with.
- Planning the sequence of events (lunch first, lunch after, no lunch . . .).
- Planning that no concessions will be made until the other party's full shopping list (all the items he or she plans to negotiate) is on the table.
- Knowing when to bring in a third-party or new negotiator.

Benefits

- Starting off WIN–WIN, as opposed to the adversarial negotiator whose strategy is to start off WIN–LOSE by opening with an extreme demand or threat, bringing extra people to the table unannounced, or keeping you waiting one hour before the negotiation.
- Presenting positive points of proposal first.
- Identifying your strengths and how you can leverage them to overcome your weaknesses.

Identify Your Essentials and Trade-Offs

Essentials are your "must haves"—terms and criteria you absolutely must have—and *trade-offs* are your items you can use to get your essentials. Your essentials constitute your output objective. At the conclusion of the negotiation, you should walk away with your essentials and unspent trade-offs (the ones you did not have to trade away) intact.

Your goal should be to keep your essentials to a minimum and expand your trade-offs to a maximum.

The more you achieve this, the easier it is to negotiate. Trade-offs give you valuable flexibility; therefore, you should be as prolific as possible in identifying them. For example, if you understand your yield, you might be able to trade 10 percent balances for a 1 percent fee. Of course, what you plan to trade must relate to what the customer needs, or it will not have *trading value*. In sorting out your essentials and trade-offs, you should consider your objective for final agreement, your needs, your customer's needs, your bottom line, and options for achieving your all-in objective.

Customers also have essentials and trade-off items and you should anticipate what they will be.

Without flexibility, the negotiation is an offer, not a negotiation. You should be prepared to *reshape* and *redesign* your proposal and be creative, innovative, and flexible to achieve a WIN–WIN agreement. You must think, "What if?" and brainstorm creative options to get around obstacles. Flexibility does not mean giving in; it means trading for value to get what you need.

Recognize Your Assumptions

As you prepare for the negotiation, it will be necessary to make assumptions. Recognize assumptions as such, and remember to test them before acting on them. If not, you will find that your own assumptions will trip you up. Assumptions are educated guesses consciously made—or, more dangerously, concepts you unconsciously take for fact. Assumptions are not facts. *The best assumption you can make is that all of your assumptions are wrong.* It is often hard to identify assumptions since they are points "taken for granted" concerning deadlines, timetables, needs, competitive offers, customer preferences, what the other side will or will not do, and so on.

Prepare Your Total Offer

Preserving price starts with understanding your price, which involves knowing your total offer. Your aim in the preparation stage should be to prepare your total offer. Your total offer is the total package—value added by the bank and you, not just dollars.

To sell your total offer you must prepare to break it down into its components, for example, industry expertise, personal commitment and attention, quality of service, innovation, delivering capability, network reliability, experience, execution, and consistency. Your total offer distinguishes your proposal from your competitors'.

The total offer concept is especially effective in demonstrating added value when you are competing against other banks that are trying to buy the business by offering below market pricing, banks that offer relatively equal deals, and banks with what appear to be *similar* products at lower rates.

Some elements of a total offer that you should consider are:

- Innovation/value added.
- Quality of service/guarantee of performance (you can deliver).
- Full spectrum products/capacity to draw on total resources/network (convenience and cost savings).
- Customizing (ability to tailor service to match in-house needs).
- State-of-the-art techniques (fewer problems).

- Attention bank management will pay to the customer.
- Staying power—"We've been there in the past, we will be there in the future."
- Reliability as a source of funds or execution.
- Relationship history—knowledge of customer's business, comfort level on *both* sides.
- Knowledge of industry.
- Consistency in the marketplace (will not withdraw in tough time).
- Global or regional network (for multinational/international customers).
- Flexibility (creativity in developing alternatives).
- Ability to move quickly, lack of bureaucracy.
- Prestige (recognized leaders—"We can get the bank group . . . .").
- Your personal commitment as the banker—YOU!
- Expertise.
- Professionalism (personalized service, experienced support people).

A total offer is the sum of all the value your bank adds to the basic product. It is a source of power and confidence. The total offer is effective with *relationship-oriented customers* and transactional customers if it shows them that it can give them what they want. While some situations are totally driven by price, these are *far fewer* than you would think. Price is overrated. Price is everything—until you connect *price* and *value*. Buyers do not look for the "cheapest" price every time they make a purchase. Quality and service, responsiveness and innovation are worth paying for in most people's books. The total offer is a way to make sure the customer knows what he or she is or is not getting.

Some situations are not really negotiations—they

are bids. For certain customers, price alone is the driving factor—not the additional value you bring through your total offer. It is important to recognize bids so that you concentrate on price and conclude the transaction expediently.

For example, a multinational company could essentially create a development deal and request project financing proposals from a group of banks. In this situation the company could be saying, "I need the money, not the bank (you), because I can structure my own deal." Customers like this, or customers who are doing a "pure" transaction such as shopping a rate for a particular swap, do not think you can add value. Unless you can change their perception of you as a provider of a commodity, price/terms *will* drive the deal. "Commodity thinking" often can be changed through the total offer approach, but if you find you're getting nowhere, price it right. If your bid is not accepted, leave the door open for a future deal.

Plan What You Will Present/Negotiate First

When negotiating several points, begin on a positive note and work on the *easiest* points first. By building a foundation of agreement early you can foster customer commitment to doing the deal. It is also important to plan what you will put on the table first and to determine which trade-off items you will use first.

By preparing to open with the positives, such as "We got the $10 million for you," and by setting a priority order for your trade-off items, you can control the negotiation and move it toward agreement. To help you maximize your trade-off items, delineate the exact order of what you plan to trade first down to what you will trade only as a last resource.

USING A NEGOTIATION ACTION PLANNER

The following Consultative Negotiation Action Planner will assist you in preparing for WIN—WIN negotiations. While the form itself as a document can be helpful, it is much more important as a *discipline* of thinking through each category. Each section is important, much more important than the small amount of space allocated to it would indicate. If two of the categories could be singled out as critical, they would be:

- Your *objective.*
- Your needs and the *needs* of the other party.

All other categories in the Consultative Negotiation Action Planner are designed to help you achieve your *objectives* and *satisfy the needs of the other party at the same time.* If you do not have a clear picture of your *desired outcome,* you cannot confidently pursue it, and without understanding the *needs* of the other party you may be a winner—or a loser—and be the last to know.

CONSULTATIVE NEGOTIATON ACTION PLANNER

Customer background:

Your needs:

Your objective for final agreement:

Your essentials (core items):   Your expendables (trade-offs):

Your customer's needs   Needs of *each* decision-maker:
Individual in decision-making unit   Product needs   Nonproduct needs

---

Your strategy:
- General strategy:
- Points to negotiate first:
- Opening terms:
- Fallback position (bottom line):
- Pricing options:
- Other ideas/factors you can bring in:

Information presented in the proposal:

Your strategy for opening the negotiation/counteropening:

Total offer elements:

Your strengths/weaknesses: | Customer's strengths/weaknesses:

Your assumptions:

Anticipated customer pressure tactics:

Deadlines/timetables:

Competition/alternatives the customer has:

Your internal resources/policy:

Conducting the Consultative Negotiation

CONSULTATIVE NEGOTIATION FRAMEWORK

By understanding the elements that make up a consultative negotiation, you can increase your awareness of what takes place during the negotiation. The more awareness you have, the greater control you have.

The consultative negotiation framework consists of:

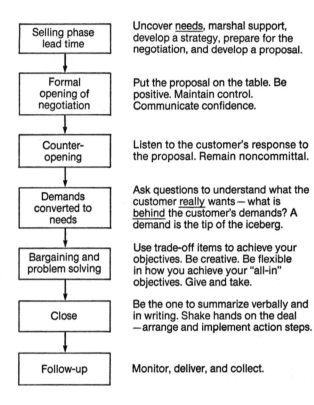

Selling phase lead time	Uncover <u>needs</u>, marshal support, develop a strategy, prepare for the negotiation, and develop a proposal.
Formal opening of negotiation	Put the proposal on the table. Be positive. Maintain control. Communicate confidence.
Counter-opening	Listen to the customer's response to the proposal. Remain noncommittal.
Demands converted to needs	Ask questions to understand what the customer <u>really</u> wants — what is <u>behind</u> the customer's demands? A demand is the tip of the iceberg.
Bargaining and problem solving	Use trade-off items to achieve your objectives. Be creative. Be flexible in how you achieve your "all-in" objectives. Give and take.
Close	Be the one to summarize verbally and in writing. Shake hands on the deal —arrange and implement action steps.
Follow-up	Monitor, deliver, and collect.

As the consultative negotiation framework is presented in this chapter, specific consultative negotiating *skills, strategies, and tactics* will also be presented.

Since selling and negotiating are part of the same continuum, the key selling skills—relating, questioning, listening, integrating, and checking—are a part of every negotiation. However, the intensity and stakes of a negotiation demand *more* from you than is required in the selling phase. Your negotiation skill can mean the difference between WIN–WIN, WIN–LOSE, LOSE– LOSE, or WALK (no deal).

The following will illustrate how the framework, skills, and tactics work together:

Consultative Negotiation Framework Elements	Your Skill	Your Strategy	Your Tactic
Customer's counter-opening	Questioning	Keep the total package in mind at all times. Get the customer's full shopping list. Convert demands to needs. Trade—do not give concessions.	Ask for the customer's full shopping list *before* making any concessions. Take notes, do not make any concessions until all the customer's demands are on the table. Be *silent* after you ask a question. Balance concessions.

OPENING THE NEGOTIATION

The negotiation is *formally* opened when the proposal—price, terms, benefits—is presented. *How* you open will make a difference in how the proposal is accepted by the other party since the confidence level you project can establish an expectation level in your customer's mind.

Power and control are established early in the negotiation process. While either party can open the negotiation, the one who puts terms on the table first usually has the advantage because he or she sets the expectation level and assumes control. There are occasions when letting the customer open is appropriate, but this usually is the exception, not the rule. In all situations, lead time should be used to identify customer needs, understand the deal parameters, and plant seeds so that your proposal does not surprise/shock your customer.

Since how you open is as or more important than what you present, you should think about your proposal as a *present* to the customer, not a bomb. To present it as a present you should begin with the positives and tie the terms you outline to customer benefits and needs. One banker who was about to ask for a very high rate on a bridge facility, opened by saying, "I am pleased—I was able to get you . . . and I also got you . . . this is the largest deal we have done together in nine years. We are looking at X percent on the bridge." While she was anticipating resistance from the customer, she was able to project confidence and got her terms. Her confidence was key to getting her objectives. If you don't believe in the fundamentals of your opening terms, you will reflect this and your customer will be quick to take advantage of your weakness.

As you present your ideas, remember to address the customer's needs and concerns. *Explain why the terms are as they are* without being defensive and continue to refer to the *benefits* to the customer. As you present opening terms, avoid giving ball park figures since your customer will automatically hear only the lower end and will hold you to it regardless of how you qualify it. For example, a customer who is told ½ to 1 hears only the ½ and disregards the 1. After you put your terms on the table, you should be quiet. Simply patiently wait for a response from your customer.

There are nuances in the opening based on who opens and what has transpired prior to the opening.

Three typical situations are:

- Opening by you with no proposal sent in advance.
- Opening by you after you have sent/presented your proposal via mail/telephone.
- Opening by the customer.

Opening by You/No Proposal Sent in Advance

When you are the one to open the negotiation, you should:

- *Build rapport.* Don't forget about the relationship factors (people to people). For example, thank the customer for the information he or she sent to you, for his or her help in formulating the proposal, or for the opportunity to look at the deal.
- *Summarize what preceded this phase. Briefly and succinctly* recap the most recent events that led to the negotiation to get agreement at the outset and establish a common ground. "Since we spoke yesterday, I have had an opportunity to work on your exposure in . . . , we can . . . ."
- *Check.* Ask if there have been any *changes* or new information since your last contact with customer. It usually is not necessary to check specific points; simply ask, "Is the situation the same?" or "Have there been any changes?" One banker who did this learned that 60 percent of the railroad his bank was financing was under water, and an investment banker discovered that his company's star research and development person was undergoing open-heart surgery! Missing this step can be *very* costly in time and money.

- *Present your proposal.* Begin in a consultative mode and present the terms and benefits of your proposal—starting with the most positive information. Be sure to *explain* how you got to these terms in a nondefensive, clear manner. Customers need to know your reasoning both for their own information and to have information to present to their managers. As you present your terms, position them relative to the customer's interests or needs and the benefits to him or her. Say, "Because of . . . (brief/nondefensive explanation), to give you . . . (benefit), *I'm* looking at . . . (opening terms)." Remember to emphasize benefits and satisfaction of customer needs as you present your proposal. Sit up straight—inch up on your chair—projecting confidence and preparation.
- *Be silent.* After you have opened, maintain *silence* and wait for your customer to respond. Again keep this in mind: *The one who speaks first after price is quoted will be the first to concede!*

Opening after You Have Sent a Proposal

When *you have sent your proposal* to your customer in advance of the meeting, in effect you have already opened and, therefore, you should *not* open again. Opening twice will weaken your position. Under these circumstances you should:

- Build rapport.
- Recap by *briefly* reviewing what led to the proposal, emphasizing areas of agreement during the selling phase.

- Check to determine if there have been any changes.
- Mention that you have sent the proposal and ask if the customer has received it/reviewed it.
- Ask for the customer's thoughts, response, and so on to the proposal rather than presenting (opening) *again. Do not discuss the proposal you sent until the customer has given you some feedback.* This process will help you maintain control.
- Listen carefully to what the customer has to say, since this is his or her counterproposal.

Opening by the Customer

In some situations, the customer will be the one to open, put his or her opening terms on the table first, or send/communicate by phone his or her proposal to you before the meeting. In this situation, you should avoid the temptation to respond with a counteroffer. You should ask questions to understand the customer's thinking and the needs that underly his or her terms. You should:

- Say you have received the proposal and summarize.

Then:

- Ask how the customer arrived at the figure (demand). Ask for more information so that you can understand the customer's thinking and needs before making a counteroffer.

This prebargaining process will be invaluable to you in several ways: It will enable you to begin to distinguish your customer's essentials and trade-offs. It will give you information you can use to position your counterproposal. It will help you develop other ways to satisfy the needs, and it will require the customer to clarify the needs behind his or her demands.

Summary of Openings

Whether you open, the customer opens, or you send a proposal in advance, all successful openings share the first three common elements: rapport, summary, and checking. The openings differ in the fourth element (presentation). When you send a proposal in advance or when your customer is the one who opens, do not present a counteropening immediately without probing. Ask questions to gain insight you can use to position your proposal and satisfy the customer's needs. All successful openings project confidence.

COUNTEROPENING

After you have presented your proposal, you should expect a counterproposal or rejection from your customer. As your customer talks you should:

- Listen.
- Stay calm. Don't let yourself be surprised, insulted, upset, or outraged.
- Sort in your mind points of agreement and points of disagreement.
- Begin to identify (make assumptions about) customer's essentials and expendables.
- Reinforce areas of agreement as soon as you hear them.

- Prepare to summarize and define *areas of agreement.*
- Get your customers *full* shopping list. (Ask, "Is there anything else . . .?")
- Test initial assumptions/ask questions.
- Begin to look for other trade-offs or alternatives that can be brought into the negotiation.

It is essential that you *get all the items for discussion out on the table* so that you can keep the total package in mind at all times. Comments such as "Let's go through all of your concerns first . . . ," "Let me make note of that point . . . ," "What else . . . so we can look at the total package," and taking notes can prevent you from making premature concessions or commitments. If you don't get the customer's full shopping list, *you may make concessions only to find that your customer wants more and more.* Once you have unearthed all of the customer's concerns/demands, you will be ready to explore them to find out the needs that motivate them.

CONVERTING DEMANDS TO NEEDS

What Does the Customer Really Need?

Negotiating is a way to get around a "no." The best way to do this is to find out what the customer's thinking is. When your customer presents a proposal or counterproposal, it is usually expressed as *demands.* Your task is to find out the needs behind the demands so that you understand his or her thinking. You can do this by asking questions. The process of understanding the needs behind the demands is essential in WIN−WIN negotiating. Demands are a fixed sum or solution. Demands are the symptoms of needs but unlike needs they are usually in conflict. Unless you can uncover needs, you risk having your negotiation deteriorate into haggling. *The key to a successful WIN—WIN negotiation is to find out what the other party really needs*, that is, what is motivating his or her demand.

If you negotiate demands, you will often find yourself "splitting the difference." Then *both* sides are apt to feel dissatisfied with a result that is less than what they want. Suppose that you and your customer disagree on rate. If your real needs are risk reduction and spread and your customer's real need is managing cash flow to meet a pay schedule, you probably can reach an agreement much more easily by looking at alternatives to satisfy those needs rather than by arguing percentage points. For example, you may consider trade-off items such as liquid collateral, marketable securities, guarantees, or add-on business—all of which can help you achieve your yield and give the other party what he or she needs. For example, for the customer who *demands* ¼:

Customer Opens: Here's the deal. I want ¼. Can you do it?	*Demand*
Banker Converts Demands to Needs: A ¼ sure would be an attractive rate. How did you arrive at that figure?	*Converting demand to need*
Customer: That's what our parent gets and we feel we should receive the same treatment. Why should we be treated differently?	*Customer's thinking behind demand*
Banker: I want to be responsive to your needs and I know that	*Trading for WIN—WIN*

is the rate X company is
getting because they are. . . .
Our thinking is that. . . . Let's
look at your. . . . What are
your thoughts on a guarantee
from X company to enable us
to meet your request?

By exploring *why* the customer is demanding ¼,
rather than giving in, saying a flat "No," or quickly
responding with a counteroffer, you may find you can
gather information that you can use to preserve your
yield or reduce your risk and give your customer what
he or she needs.

Unless you identify needs you may find that "splitting the difference" will be a knee-jerk reaction. You
may also find that you left money on the table because
you didn't take all the elements of the deal into consideration. Avoid becoming glued to positions and blind to
opportunities. Ask "Why?" and think, "What if?" before
and during the negotiation.

In the short story "Gift of the Magi," by O. Henry,
the wife cuts her hair to buy her husband a watch fob
and her husband sells his watch to buy her a comb.
Their *failure to communicate* led to *unnecessary sacrifice* on both sides.

Asking Questions to Identify Needs

Asking questions seems to be extremely difficult for
many negotiators. There is a feeling that negotiators
who ask questions will seem unprepared or weak in their
positions. Nothing could be further from the truth. Questions are the power tools of negotiating. They help you

maintain control. They help you move the negotiation forward. They help you stand firm. They help you put the onus on the other party to explain his or her thinking behind the demand. And they give you information and insight you need to get around a customer's "No."

The ability to question in a nonhostile way is essential in successful negotiating in a competitive marketplace.

The following example will illustrate the value of asking a question. After the banker presented his proposal, the customer emphatically replied, "That's unacceptable!" Many negotiators would have proceeded to defend the terms they just proposed. In most situations, however, it is infinitely more powerful to ask, as this banker did, "Why do you find it unacceptable?" He then maintained silence. By asking "Why?" the negotiator gained information and insight into the customer's thinking and needs. He got ammunition he could use to get through the objection/tactic and he conveyed a willingness to listen. Because the banker asked "Why?" the customer responded, "My budget . . . . I can't go to senior management now." The parties then worked out a way to stage the delivery of the service for two months to meet the budget requirements. The customer got his system and the banker protected his profitability.

The same kind of question is effective with the customer who says, "I won't sign personally." Customers are not interested in hearing about your institution's policy. Whether the objection is genuine or is a tactic, your task is to find a way around it. So rather than explaining to them about the *policy*, you can ask them "Why?" they won't sign. Then you can use what they tell you to advance your position or possibly change your position.

Rather than making you appear weak, asking questions enables you to show confidence. Questions can save you from haggling. With the answers to your questions you can be creative and persuasive.

It takes discipline, self-confidence, and patience to ask questions, but learning to use "Why?" throughout the negotiation pays tremendous dividends.

Use questions to:

- Convert demands to needs—"Why?"
- Get the customer's full shopping list (before you begin to convert demands to needs)—"You mentioned there were several points. What else is of concern to you?" "Anything else?"
- Uncover new information—"Have there been any changes since we spoke yesterday morning?"
- Keep the negotiation on track—"At this point I think we have five outstanding issues. They are . . . . Is that right?" or "Can we table that and get back to it after . . . ?"
- Control an adversarial negotiator—"What are you looking for? 95 is only .05 away from the historical spread."

  Customer: The spread is not wide enough.

  Banker: What are you looking for?

- Avoid customer pressure tactics:

  Customer: We have to get this done by 5 P.M. today.

  Banker: What is the timetable? or Why is that?

- Guard against being manipulated by requiring customers to explain/defend vague, unsupported, or irrational statements—"Do you have a firm commitment?"

- Define tactics:

Customer: You said between $12 and $18 an item and now you come back on the high end at $18. I resent that.

Banker: I have no recollection of the $12 quotation. When do you feel you heard this from me? (Banker's hand points to his well-documented notes and file.)

- Exiting from an unprofitable relationship—"How do you rank us among your banks?"

Once you ask a question, you must maintain *silence* and steadily and *patiently* wait for an answer.

Questions are so powerful that some customers will try to evade them. When they do this, *repeat* the question. You may use different words, but you must go after the same information.

In summary, question can be used to uncover the *needs* behind *demands*. Most importantly, they will help you control the situation, keeping you armed with information and on the offensive rather than the defensive.

BARGAINING

Introduction

The bargaining phase is the time to *trade*. Once you have your customer's full shopping list and understand needs, you are ready to bargain. When bargaining as a consultative negotiator, you, too, will use tactics. The difference between an adversarial negotiator and a consultative negotiator is a matter of pattern, degree, and objective: *how* you negotiate, *how* far you go, and *what* you wish to accomplish. Many of the bargaining tactics you will use when negotiating with another consultative negotiator will be similar to the ones you use to control an adversarial. And some of the tactics you use will be identical to those used by the adversarial—such as silence. However, as a consultative negotiator you should avoid the *adversarial* tactics such as extreme demands. Consultative tactics are legitimate and effective ways to reach your objectives and help move the negotiation along. The difference in tactics is truly a matter of extremes, degree, and objective for final outcome. For example, in basketball, fouls are penalized but they are accepted as a strategic part of the game. Elbows can be used; clubs cannot!

During the bargaining phase, you need to be fully prepared to discuss and work with your proposal. It is essential that you fully understand your own proposal and that you be as prepared as possible with as many figures and options as you can generate. You should also talk about your proposal from the customer's point of view—how it will benefit him or her. The customer is doing business with you in order to achieve a particular set of benefits. Therefore, as you bargain, position your trade-offs as a way to help you and your customer achieve the benefits you both seek.

Build Agreement

Among the most important tactics for reaching a final WIN—WIN agreement are:

- Starting off with positives—"We're agreed on the $100,000 fee." "We got the approval."
- Using areas of agreement to help get over rough spots—"I think there are some good principles for proceeding . . . . I'd like to propose . . . that would follow in concept with your plan but would . . . ," or "You indicated there was some flexibility. . . . I need . . . ."
- Holding the difficult issues until later when a foundation of agreement on other points has been established—"Let's put that aside. . . ."
- Trading and giving nondefensive explanations— "We've requested prime + 1 and you are requesting sub-prime. We should be getting prime + 1. Because of . . . I can cut back to prime + ½ by looking at increasing . . . to give you . . . ."
- Maintaining relationships by being hard on issues and easy on people—"I have confidence in your management and that is why . . . ."

Once you find yourself faced with areas of disagreement, you can continue to convert demands to needs (this is a process used throughout the negotiation) and to trade. When the give-and-take process reaches an impasse you can *table* area(s) of disagreement. You could say, "We agree on the amount and the term, let's table the rate for now and move on to fees for X . . . ." In this way you can create a total offer which, on balance, gives the customer what he or she needs and helps you keep the negotiation moving forward.

It is very important that you identify agreements, verbalize them, and use them to *reinforce* forward motion and agreement. You can also use comments of encouragement, especially when you hit an impasse. You should reinforce areas of agreement by saying, "We have agreed on . . . , tell me what's disturbing you about . . . ," or "We both want to do this deal, what if . . .?" or "We're going to do this deal . . . , let's . . . ," "I want to accept your deal in your concept but I need some compromise." These comments of reinforcement can help get through obstacles. Visualize yourself building a bridge, brick by brick. Each time you reach a point of agreement and *verbalize* it, you lay one more brick.

There are certain phrases you should avoid because they often make things blow up. For example, while you can be firm on a given point, you should avoid actually saying the words, "Take it or leave it," or (almost never) "*Absolutely* not!" Think about what you say and how you say it. You have to live with it—and just might have to retreat from it.

Look for Ways to Satisfy Needs

Bargaining calls for creativity. You must look for and create ways to satisfy the needs of the other side while protecting your objectives. A successful negotiator is a creative negotiator. Creativity means devising options that you can present to the customer. Many different combinations of these options can add up to give you your "yield" and satisfy your objective.

It can also be very useful to try to accept your customer's structure or concept for a particular deal, but suggest a compromise on the terms. For example, if a merger and acquisition customer wants to tie the fee to performance, you could accept the principle but say, "I think the idea to create a sliding scale fee is something we can do. However, we would need $7 million as the base fee."

In addition to using options, you should continue

to identify variables, that is, items that were not thought of as negotiable either because they seemed nonnegotiable or because no one thought of them before. By identifying new items that were not previously included in either party's original thinking, you can expand the negotiating field. For example, a deal was about to deadlock because of what seemed to be an irresolvable difference. The treasurer of a subsidiary of a large corporation demanded lower than market pricing; however, to agree to this, the banker required a guarantee from the parent that the parent was unwilling to give because of board restrictions. The treasurer would not bend on the rate (he wanted to look good) and the banker could not agree on the rate without the guarantee (he needed protection and assurances of repayment). Almost at a point of deadlock the banker found a new *variable*: The customer pledged his *timberlands*, which no one had previously considered.

Check for Agreement and Understanding

Another important negotiating tactic is checking. *During a negotiation you must not be led into thinking that silence means agreement.* During the bargaining phase, you should check for agreement and understanding to keep track of what has and has not been agreed to. Unless you do this incrementally, you may think that a particular point has been settled when it has not. Customers may sit quietly and listen to your terms, hoping that you will *assume* they agree. Of course, later they will be quick to point out they in fact had *not* agreed. Since this mistake can be very costly to you, check everything by asking, "Are we then agreed on . . . ," or

"What do you think?" You should be silent and wait for a reply. Or you can be assumptive by confidently saying, "Good, then we agree on. . . . Is this right?" Checking will enable you to gauge your position and make decisions on how and when to use trade-offs and how to pace the negotiation.

Checking will help you tabulate points of agreement, identify and weigh points of disagreement, and head off possible deadlocks by allowing you to switch gears.

In a negotiation, checking is a double-edged sword. In general, it is a valuable practice but there is one time when you should *not* check. Instead, you should be absolutely silent. This is when you state price/terms. Silence will say more about your resolve than any eloquence.

Resolve Objections

A negotiation can be considered a series of objections, a process for getting around the word *no*. Objections can easily lead to conflict. How you deal with objections can intensify the conflict or resolve it. Working through objections is achieved by what you say and, more importantly, how you say it. During a negotiation, expect customers to object to price and terms.

Oscar Wilde defined a cynic as "someone who knows the price of everything and the value of nothing." If this is true, then most customers are cynics. They need to be reminded of the value associated with price. For most customers, that value—value added by you, possibly over what your competitors can do—is worth paying for. First and foremost, you have to understand and believe in the value (total offer) of what you bring to the table, and then you have to be able to present that value in a plausible and convincing way.

Price is more than a number. Price is the answer in an equation. *Price is the sum total of history, knowledge, and confidence.* As you bargain, you should expect price and term objections. When customers object to price and terms they are really looking to you to justify the *value*, not give in. They expect you to be able to *justify* the price and help them feel confident that your price is right. While customers hammer away at price or a particular term, they are equally concerned about such things as execution, service, peace of mind, and so on.

As you work to preserve your price, one way you can help to justify your figure is by discussing a *unique* aspect of the particular deal such as:

- Size—"That's for $1 million versus $50 million . . . ."
- Credit aspects—"This is not a liquid piece of paper . . . ."
- Market environment—"the market is in a downturn . . . , your industry is such you can't expect those rates . . . ," or "Rates have gone up."
- Value added—industry expertise, knowledge of customer (total offer).

Customers expect you to trade with them—to negotiate, *not* cave in. When they object to price, they are testing your ability to preserve and defend the terms. In a negotiation the customer will test you—test your reasoning, your credibility, your stamina, your conviction, and your courage. The *worst* thing to do when the other party says, "It's too high," is to give in without asking questions or trading to achieve your objective. If you say, "We take balances" before you really know how deep or valid the price objection is, you will destroy your own credibility as well as hurt your profits. Worse, you probably still will not have satisfied your customer.

Negotiating effectively boils down not to who has the best price, but who can successfully negotiate the change in price between what the customer demands and what you/your institution demands. Dealing effectively with price negotiation requires that you (1) know your deal and its worth to the customer, (2) present it in the most effective and convincing way, and (3) convert demands to needs and creatively work at satisfying needs.

The following Objection Resolution Model will help you present your rationale and preserve your price and terms to conclude WIN–WIN agreements. It will help you stand firm and not cave in, jump in with a counteroffer, or dig your heels in with a flat "No" before you understand why and what the customer is saying.

Four-Part Objection Resolution Model

1. *Empathize* by repeating the objection—"I know you are really growing and that is great." (Keep the relationship level positive; show empathy and respect for the customer's view.)
2. *Question* to clarify—"So I can understand what your thinking is, tell me, how did you arrive at the $20 million figure?"
3. *Present*—After you *listen* to the customer you will be in a good position to present your ideas in a persuasive way since you can focus on need satisfaction. For example, you may find the customer needs $7 million over the next 10 months and that you can meet his or her needs and meet

your standards. As you present the features and benefits of your deal, use your total offer.

4. *Check*—Ask what the customer thinks about what you have presented. Check for agreement and understanding to determine if the objection has been resolved. (Second warning: When you are stating price, you should *not* check, you should be silent.)

In responding to the "too high rate/fee" objection or any such comparative ("too," "not . . . enough") you should say, "I know you want to get the best deal possible, *but to what are you comparing us in thinking this is too high?*"

The fundamental *clarifying questions* in a negotiation are always the same—"What are you *comparing* this to?" or "How did you arrive at that?"

You should either uncover what you are being compared to or you should find out *why* the customer is making a particular demand.

Especially in a competitive situation, you must look behind the competitor's price that your customer alludes to. If you can get the customer to be specific, you frequently can preserve your price by comparing and contrasting deals, differences, and by pointing out what the customer may be risking in going with the other offer. You may find that for a lower price, the customer is sacrificing the essentials that he or she needs. You may also find that the customer has failed to tell you what else the competitor is demanding. For example, a customer may tell you "X bank wants a $100,000 fee" when you are asking for $300,000. The Objection Resolution Model will give you a process for making sure you understand all that is involved in the other offer. It will assist you in finding out from the customer what he or she is getting for the $100,000 and what other fees, other business, terms, and so on he or she may be providing to your competitor to compensate for the fee, allowing the competitor to offer particular terms. It will assist you in comparing offers *side by side*, making sure *you and your customer* understand all the parts of each institution's offer.

The Objection Resolution Model provides you with a way to find out what you are being compared to (looking beyond price) and gives you a format for presenting your total offer—the particular features and benefits of the proposal, the quality, and the total value added, such as track record and execution or network and expertise. Preserving price can often be achieved by discussing your total offer and making comparisons— comparing apples with apples.

While price is important, it is *just one* of the factors in many customers' decisions to buy. It is not everything. It is far from everything. Value (trust and confidence) is often more important. Recently, when a group of corporate customers were asked why they selected their tennis rackets, not one chose the racket because it was the cheapest. Several said they selected theirs because it was the *most* expensive. No one in the group was surprised by the outcome of this informal study, yet the seller frequently thinks price is everything. In most situations, if you can add value or satisfy the buyer's real needs, the buyer will pay for it, will often pay a premium, and will walk away satisfied.

The total offer will help you link price with value. Price is relative and this is appreciated not only by "relationship-oriented" customers but also by what look like transactional or bid customers. The total offer will help them understand what they are getting or risking by not doing the deal or buying the product from you.

An excellent example of preserving price and the

antithesis of *price panic* is that of the banker who asked his long-standing customer for prime + 1. When the middle market customer complained, saying anyone would give him the money at prime, the banker replied, "Fine, I'll walk you down the hall and introduce you to someone in this bank who will probably give it to you at prime. But you call me on Sunday nights. You asked me to save your business when the chips were down . . . ." The customer paid prime + 1. While this may seem like an extreme situation, this banker demonstrated that he knew what he was worth. And by confidently asking for it, he got it! One investment banker says he preserves price based on value by asking his customers who threatened to go to a competitor/newcomer to a particular type of business, "If you needed a brain surgeon, would you shop price?"

If you do not understand your pricing/terms, or if you feel they are not competitive, you should make your concerns known internally. Provide your managers with the feedback and hard data to support the lost business you attribute to uncompetitive pricing (relative to value). If you don't believe in your pricing, you will find yourself negotiating *more* with your institution than with your customer. This tell-tale sign should point you to two action steps: (1) study your pricing rationale and total offer, (2) apply your knowledge in a consultative negotiation manner. When a customer says, "You'll have to give us better pricing," you should recognize that the customer is likely using a *tactic* and that your role is to counter it, not give in.

State Price Confidently

In today's competitive environment, you may get bombarded with "Your rate is too high," "Your fees are too high," or "Your terms are too inflexible." This constant barrage of resistance can be demoralizing, making you feel apologetic and insecure, if you let it. You can begin to believe such reactions even when they are mistaken. But remember, they are often knee-jerk reactions on a customer's part.

To maintain confidence in your pricing, keep in mind that a particular deal might reap great profits for the customer. For this reason, it is helpful for you to know as soon as possible the return the customer is expecting on the deal. This knowledge can put the deal in perspective for you and prevent you from succumbing to fear of losing the deal.

Throughout the bargaining phase you must communicate that you believe in your proposal/pricing. You can be successful in getting your fees if you have the *confidence* and knowledge that your deal is worth it. You can project confidence by your presence:

- Sit up, inch up on your chair as you present price.
- Speak up, keep your voice steady.
- Look at your customer.

Don't pause and don't raise your voice at the end of your sentence since that says to the customer, "I'm asking for your permission" rather than "I believe in this pricing." Your body language is also important. Keep your head straight, since a tilted head says "Please be easy on me." Preface the price with a *benefit* related to satisfying the customer's needs and exhibit confidence in what you present. Look at your customer, keeping steady eye contact. State your price/terms confidently. You can *sandwich* the price between two benefits but after you state price remain *silent*.

Concession Tactics (Reducing/Changing Price and Terms)

During a negotiation, you may find it necessary to make concessions regarding your proposal. Your objective in making a concession is to reach your objectives and help the customer reach his or hers.

The following general principles can help you maximize the benefits both parties can gain from concessions:

Trade Concessions: Do Not Give Them Away. Use trade-offs strategically. Trade-offs provide the give-and-take aspect of negotiation and should be used by you *to acquire essentials.* Trading is a way to reach agreement *without* giving in! Concessions presented as "What if?" can help lead to mutually acceptable agreements. Use your concessions to give you flexibility and trade for equal value. The only time to give something away is if it is a planned tactic (goodwill gesture) on your part to set a collaborative tone with a negotiator. Never make the first major concession with an adversarial negotiator. Every time you are about to make a concession ask yourself, "What can I get back?"

Get Your Customer's Full Shopping List before Making a Concession. Customers often make demands one at a time. Your objective should be to get your customer's full shopping list of demands on the table so you know the full scope of the proposal before you begin to trade concessions. Negotiating without seeing the full menu is like jumping into a swimming pool without knowing the depth of the water. If you deal with each item one at a time as it comes up instead of getting the full picture, you are apt to make too many concessions.

When a customer tries to "nibble," say, "I understand you are interested in X. You mention there were a few other points of concern. Let's look at what else you feel is important before . . . ," or "Let me make note of that. What else is of concern so that we can look at the total package?"

You must keep your eye on the total package and avoid making *piecemeal* agreements/commitments until you understand the customer's total menu of demands. Watch out for phrases like, "Just a few small points," "You can do that small thing, can't you?"

In making concessions, you must keep the big picture in mind and help your customer do the same. In team negotiations, one team player should keep track of concessions on both sides. If you are negotiating on your own, you should be careful to keep track of both your customer's concessions and your own.

Make Concessions Slowly and in Decreasing Increments. Especially when you reduce your price, do so in a credible manner. Find out *why* (in comparison to what) a price/term is being considered too high/unacceptable *before ever considering reducing price or changing terms.* But when you lower your price, do so *slowly* and in *diminishing increments,* to maintain credibility and control customer expectations about further concessions. When you make a concession, trade it by getting something in return. This will not only help keep things in balance but it will also increase the customer's perception of the value of the concession.

In negotiating, it is not only *what* you do, but *how* and *when* you do it that makes a difference. Nowhere is this more true than when making concessions. Your concession behavior will indicate to the other side how much more you have to give and how much further you can be pushed. When dealing with adversarial negotiators, make almost imperceptible concessions and get something of equal value back.

"Change the Price, Change the Deal."   When you are considering changing price, look for what you can take out or what you can put into the deal. By having "change the price, change the deal" as your motto, you will maintain your credibility. Whether your rationale for the concession is changing terms or conditions, adding or subtracting, or reconsidering value of the full relationship, you should be able to justify your concession or the new terms of your agreement. Often you can justify the change because of new information or a change somewhere else in the deal. For example, a banker was able to credibly reduce her prime plus ½ rate to prime, the rate offered by a competitor, by changing the term of the loan. The other bank had offered a shorter term, and substituting this term made the lower rate more acceptable. Another banker gave a private banking client, a CEO, the corporate rate that his company was getting but also got *all* of the customer's personal investments. You must look for variables such as additional business or longer or shorter term that will give you what you need and give the customer what he or she needs. If your price is higher, you are probably offering more value and should be paid for it.

Quantify (Use Your Calculator!).   If the customer asks you to lower your rate by, for example, ½, convert the ½ to what it means in total dollars and cost to you. If you negotiate the ½, it might seem like a small amount, but what it works out to in total may change your perception; so negotiate the $10,000, $20,000, or $100,000 rather than the ½ percent. Avoid working the calculations out for the *first time* in front of the customer since the results must not be in your favor. If the difference is very small, say $3,000, and the customer says, "If it is so *small* why don't you eat it?" say, "Because *that* represents my profit. In the context of the whole deal, this is not the case for you."

Make Each Concession Count.   Make a big deal over a concession. Do not make light of a concession or it will lose its trading value in the customer's eyes. Avoid saying, "Oh, we can easily do that," or "Oh, that's nothing, sure." One negotiator says that he makes a point *not to smile* when he makes a concession with anyone. Moreover, this negotiating pro advises his younger people not to smile *too* happily at the *end* of any negotiation because customers may feel they could have gotten more, and may decide to reopen or go for more for the next go-round.

How you concede is more important than *what* you concede because concessions are both *emotionally* and *financially satisfying.* Concessions give the customer more than money. They give the customer *satisfaction* and a feeling he or she got a good deal. Customers feel better when they work for concessions. Satisfying dollar needs alone will not satisfy the customer because a price need is *not* the same as price demand.

People focus on money because it is quantifiable and is a way to keep score. Real needs are seldom what they seem to be ("I only care about the price") because people don't express their nonproduct needs and sometimes they don't recognize their own needs. Lowering a price will not necessarily satisfy the customer. In fact, it can cause a customer to devalue your proposal ("You get what you pay for"). Therefore, you should allow the customer to work for (trade) his or her concession so that the customer *gains satisfaction* from the concession and feels satisfied by the agreement.

Avoid Even-Increment Mentality. Concessions do not have to be in equivalent increments. Don't get trapped into thinking in the same increments as your customer. For example, if the fee is $45,000 and your customer offers $35,000, don't automatically think in terms of $5,000 blocks. See the alternatives between the blocks. For example, rather than go to $40,000, go to $43,000.

Watch How You Phrase It (No Ultimatums). As you make concessions or do not make concessions, be careful of what you say and how you say it. Watch phrases such as, "final offer ...," or "if you don't accept this ...." It is important to leave yourself room for retreat. It is more useful to say, "This is the best we can do," "I need to do this," or "If you can't do ..., I need to pass."

Guard against Making Deadline Concessions. The time to *pay special attention* to concessions is when the *deadline* nears and major points are conceded out of panic. Adversarial negotiators will patiently wait you out, so avoid making a big concession at the deadline. Deadline concessions are for the other party: Take them, but don't make them.

Be Creative in Generating Possible Concessions. When you become blocked in a negotiation, expand the universe of tradable items by creatively developing options or exploring variables not previously considered.

In summary, concessions are an important part of negotiating. They give you flexibility and help you get what you want. Therefore, you should plan your concessions carefully and make them strategically.

Tactics for Preserving Price/Terms

In addition to concession tactics, there are specific consultative tactics that can be used in the *bargaining phase* to *preserve price*. While many of these tactics have been covered previously, it may be helpful to list them together as price holders.

Silence. Use silence after you state your price, because first to speak is first to concede! If you talk after you quote price you may talk yourself into a concession. Patience is truly a virtue when you negotiate. Silence says to the customer that you are confident. Be prepared to withstand the silent treatment from your customer. Use the time to think, observe your customer, and evaluate the situation. Also be silent after you ask a question, whenever your customer makes an outrageous or inappropriate comment, and whenever you need to establish control or to think.

Shopping List. Get your customer's full menu of demands before negotiating price.

Get Specific. Examine the numbers before the negotiation. Show what the difference boils down to. Prepare indicative numbers if you can't present actual figures. One banker convinced his customer to pay a $5,000 fee when he spelled out the overall annual savings to the customer with the instrument. The fee was dwarfed by the six-figure savings. Say, "Let's look at what X means," and work out the figures. Of course, make sure you know *beforehand* how the calculations will work out. Quantify. Ask, "How many are we talking about?" Use unit pricing or bundle/unbundle pricing. By breaking price into smaller units you can often point out the cost/value ratio.

Get Off Price.　Convert customer price demands to customer needs.

Set and Keep Your Aspiration Level High.　There is a startling correlation between expectations and results. Set your sights high and don't allow the adversarial negotiator to shift them to a lower target level.

Side by Side.　When your customer refers to "a better offer," find out what specifically is included in it. Don't allow the customer to focus on just one aspect of a competitive deal. Customers may try to "cherry pick" on price or terms by isolating one point of your proposal and comparing it with a competitor's. They could be doing this to mislead you. They also may not fully understand what the total package will cost them. Your job is to keep the total package in mind and compare offers only when you know the total packages under consideration. You should ask for specifics on the other offers and options, since few packages are exactly alike. Your aim should be to make sure you and your customer are comparing apples and apples. You should find out:

- What are the details of the competitive offer? What else are they *giving, getting?*
- Can we look at the proposals side by side since the *total* deals may be different?
- Create competition for yourself. Show confidence.

Show Confidence. Mask any signs of panic. As the commercial says, "Never let them see you sweat!" Project confidence and conviction. Don't be tentative as you speak. Watch your body language. Don't clasp your hands together in an imploring manner when you present price or a term that you know the customer will initially reject. Be sure to maintain eye contact. Shifting away eyes or looking downward can communicate tentativeness and fear. Be thoughtful, well-paced, and self-assured. Preparation, self-image, and experience create confidence. As you present price, keep your voice strong and look the customer in the eye. Straighten your back ever so slightly or inch up in the chair. Have *presence* when you present your proposal.

OTHER CONSULTATIVE TACTICS

The following additional consultative tactics will help you create WIN—WIN deals:

Personalize the Deal. Use "I" rather than the name of the bank/firm or the royal "we" at critical times in the negotiation. It will show confidence and demonstrate that you not only believe in your proposal but that you are accountable for it. "I" is more persuasive than, "Bank of X needs . . . ." Instead say, "I've . . . , and I think . . . ."

Ask "Why" (Negotiate Needs, Not Demands). Don't be afraid to ask *questions*. Asking "Why" will help you understand your customer's *needs*. It will also allow you to test for adversarial or consultative tactics. When customers make a demand, you should ask the customer to explain why he or she thinks that way rather than arguing the point with him or her. For example, you could ask, "How did you arrive at that?" or you can say, "What specifically is in the offer made to you by X firm?" Questioning and listening are keys to uncovering underlying needs.

Test All Assumptions. Things are rarely as they appear during a negotiation. Therefore test and question all of your assumptions about what the other side will or will not do or accept. Question all general statements and closely scrutinize "facts." Formulate assumptions before the negotiation and then assume that all of your assumptions are *wrong* until you have *tested* each one.

Begin in a Consultative Manner. Even with a WIN–LOSE negotiator, begin in a consultative mode. Ask "Why;" Don't make concessions, but don't attack. Your greatest weapons are your knowledge of what you will and will *not* accept and your ability to walk away from a WIN–LOSE deal.

Take Notes. Take notes during the negotiation. This will help you keep track of what is going on. It will give you the "record" you may need later when the customer says, "but we agreed to . . . ." It will help you table items. For example, you could say, "Let me make note of that. Can we move on to . . . and not get bogged down . . . , keep this to the side . . . ." It will spare you from making concessions before you have the customer's full menu of demands. It will also help you keep track of *concessions* on all sides.

Use Repetition. You should repeat benefits *again* and

again. You should repeat your needs and position over and over. Persistance and repetition will help persuade the customer. It will say to the customer, "My banker really believes in this." Also ask questions again that the customer has not answered. Restate the same ideas again and again to make a point.

Delay Issues/Table It. Phrases such as "Let me think about that," "I'd like to check this out further," "Let me make a note of that," and "I'll get back to you on it" are *essential* when you are not prepared to make a commitment and need time to plan a new strategy or get interpretation on a policy, and so on. Of course, you should not miss a hot opportunity, but you should not commit unless you can live with the commitment.

When you reach an impasse, it is useful to table the topic that is creating an obstacle and move to the other points. For example, a fee of X may become the deal breaker. Say, "Let's put that aside and move on to . . . ." Often agreement on all other areas, consideration of the value of the total package to either side, or consideration of other areas for concessions will help resolve the problem with the fee.

Never Say "Never!"—Play for Time. Rather than say, "Never!" or "Absolutely not!" unless you are prepared to deadlock, say, "I would like to give this some thought," or "I need to go over these figures," or "This doesn't look good. . . . Let me make a note. . . . Let's move on to . . . ." Time is a great tactic because customers use it! If you don't, your customer will.

Be Patient. Extreme patience is called for during a negotiation. You must take your time. Time can be the *most powerful* factor you have as a negotiator.

Be Flexible. Build "what if's" into your proposal so that you can trade. The more *trade-offs* you have, the more flexibility. Limit your essentials and be prepared to guard them. Use the concept of "total yield," the elements that combine to make up your objective, to increase your flexibility.

Nail Down the Future. Don't fall victim to a promise for future profits. Customers may say, "You know early next year we will be . . . financing . . . and we'd like you to look at that . . . . There are opportunities for substantial *future* business here." Generally speaking, settling for a WIN—LOSE in exchange for a promise of future gains is not good business. Good relationships are built on WIN—WINs from the start. WIN—LOSE relationships usually don't last very long because the LOSE side is not satisfied. If you determine that for very specific reasons the future deal or even a part of the deal warrants consideration, *pinpoint* the *specific future* piece of business and time frame. Changes in personnel and policy are all too common, so confirm this in writing to increase the possibility that the promise will be honored by the negotiator and his or her company. In general, do not let customers negotiate the future with you.

Plant Seeds Early. Control your customer's expectation level by giving indications early about what is or is not possible. If you feel a request or demand that the customer is making is most probably not possible because of internal guidelines, and so on, say, "I understand you want . . . . I would like you to know that we usually do not have an appetite for this . . . ," or "We're not in the same ball park *at all* on this . . . but I will look into it . . . and get back to you on . . . ." (Slightly shake your head, "No.") Explore all possibilities and then if the request is not possible, get back to the customer *without* delay.

Use Limited Authority to Your Advantage. You can use limited authority as self-protection. It can help you avoid making hasty, premature commitments and give you a fallback position. It may seem like a fine line but you must convey limited authority (when you need it) and still maintain full accountability. If you shift the accountability to "them," the customer will want to speak with "them," not you. Remember, no one has unlimited authority. Say, "I want to bring this back so we (not they) can review it in depth."

Avoid "Attacking Face" at All Costs. "Attacking face," never a good move in private, is especially damaging in public (in the presence of a third party). It is a *serious relationship mistake*, since people will "keep score" and "get even" whenever they have a chance if they feel they have been humiliated or embarrassed in front of others. Saving face is important in all situations. A part of saving face is letting the other party win something, particularly letting an adversarial negotiator win something.

Go "Off the Record." Saying that a particular comment/idea is "off the record" while lowering your voice can be a useful tactic for *getting closer* to the customer and informally testing out ideas. It can be very helpful during a break or as an aside to test ideas and send up a "trial balloon" to determine how far the other side is willing to go. Another way to create the special off-the-record climate is to write an idea on a piece of paper and give it to an intermediary, such as your customer's lawyer. If it is acceptable, the customer's lawyer can be your advocate by presenting the idea for you. However, remember that no matter what is said, *nothing is ever really off the record in a negotiation.*

Draw on the Strength of Your Organization. Your institution's prestige is a powerful tool. You should show support and *respect* for your institution and your colleagues if you are to draw on this strength. *Do not* "side with the customer" against your institution because it will backfire on you. United you stand . . . .

Use One Reason (Argument) at a Time. Use one reason, point, or argument at a time when supporting your position. This will maximize the influence and advantage you can gain from each point. If you clump all of your reasons together you will not have points to use in round two.

Recognize the Significance of Changes. Expect changes. React clearly and swiftly to all surprises. New information, new people, new economic conditions, or any shift in power should be viewed as the *tip of the iceberg.* It is important to observe, respond, probe deeply, listen, and change accordingly.

Maintain Balance. You should avoid being too harsh or too easy. Customers do not value things that come too easily, but they resent terms and negotiators that are too hard.

Observe Nonverbal Signals. Nonverbal cues can give you important insights and information and supplement what you gather from a verbal exchange with your customer. Of course, there can be a danger in drawing assumptions from nonverbal cues and body language. Unless you know the person well and have had an opportunity to observe repetitive mannerisms, you may incorrectly assign a meaning. Observations must be tested gently with questions before being acted upon.

Some behaviors, such as arms crossed over the chest (closed off, guarded), rubbing of the nose (dislike for what was just said or what just transpired), lock-horns seating (seated across from one another and ready to take the other side on), hands behind one's head with elbows out (disengaging) are particularly meaningful at the negotiation table. For example, if a customer makes a disengaging gesture, ask yourself, "Is that a signal that he or she just got what he or she wanted?" and test hard. After *observing* and *testing*, use your skills and tactics to *act on the signals* based on your judgment.

Follow Up.　After you present your proposal, don't just hope that it will work out. Remember, you should not wait for the phone to ring. *Call* the customer one day after you present your proposal. You can say, "I'm calling to see if you had any further questions." After that you can say, "What reactions . . . , any concerns . . . ?" *It is very important to make this call.* While you don't want to sound too hungry or overeager, you should convey *interest*, especially when you are high(er) priced. Invariably you will learn something that will give you an edge during the remainder of the negotiation and will help you fine-tune your strategy.

CLOSING THE NEGOTIATION

The objective of the consultative approach is to close

WIN–WIN deals. When you have an agreement, you should be the one to summarize so that you can express the agreement in your own terms and from your own perspective. You should recap the terms agreed upon and then write up the agreement. As in any legal agreement, the party that writes the contract has the advantage. By being the one to do this, you can *position the understanding from your perspective* and ensure that each party leaves with the *same* understanding of what has transpired and what is to follow. Of course, whatever is written should be composed with the idea that it may ultimately be used in litigation! As you reach a WIN–WIN agreement, you should follow up and act quickly to wrap it up. Procrastination can cost the deal because of changes inside the company or among competitors. Of course, you should commit to action steps only when you are certain you have internal commitment and when you are satisfied that the agreement is attractive for your bank. Remember, you are *not* expected to make decisions on the spot. It is better to delay than to make a hasty, premature, or bad agreement. But once you do reach an agreement, summarize it and act on it!

Deadlocks

There will be situations in which you will reach an impasse after you have explored all known options. A deadlock or serious dissatisfaction on one or both sides is not to anyone's advantage. Deadlocks are usually losing situations. If compromises were never made, business would stop. This is a pressure both you and your customers are always under.

Avoiding/Breaking Deadlocks

A true deadlock occurs only when one or both sides have changed positions so that the deal or agreement is no longer possible. As this occurs, be sure not to scorch the bridges you have built. A deadlock does not mean it is over. Again, "It ain't over 'til it's over," that is, the customer gets the loan or does the deal somewhere else. Deadlocks can be unlocked *only if one side goes back to the other.* Of course, it is usually preferable for the other side to make the overture, but when this does not happen, you can initiate the contact. Do not let your ego get in the way of reopening the negotiation. On the other hand, be selective in what you say and how you say it when you break a deadlock, so that, if necessary, you can credibly and professionally retreat back into it to gain more time.

To *avoid* a deadlock:

- Don't panic. Mask your fear. Remember "It ain't over . . . ."
- *Take a break* (buy time, go back to the drawing board). Caucus. Recess. Reevaluate.
- *Postpone* difficult items for later. For example: if $A + B + C + D + E$ = deal, and you will have probable agreement on all but B and E, save B and E for last.
- Don't allow a deadlock without asking, "Why?"
- Allow for acceptance time.
- Change negotiators and/or level of negotiators, for example, bring in your manager *and/or* the customer's.
- Change time or location.
- Find a simple solution: split the difference, share and share alike, round the numbers.

- Look for or restate areas of agreement.
- Look for new variables to add in or restructure what you already have.
- Keep an eye on the total package.
- Change the formula: Change the shape of the deal (take off blinders and be creative).
- Go "off the record."
- View the deadlock as an opportunity for creative problem solving.
- Genuinely care, but don't care too much. Be able to walk.
- Try new phrases, such as "This . . . is pivotal. Can we do it in this way?"

Accepting a Deadlock

Although some "deadlocks" are arranged on purpose because there is a change of policy or circumstances, many are created by genuine, irresolvable differences that cannot be overcome. In situations like these, the negotiation should be terminated without burning bridges. Breaking off a negotiation should be calm and friendly, since paths are apt to cross in the future. Also, with present customers you must be careful not to damage your present relationship or close down future opportunities. As you accept the deadlock, be sure to do it in a way that saves face for both sides and keeps the door open, for example, "We have really tried to work this out . . . circumstances are such . . . hopefully another time . . . ."

The Exit Close

The exit close, walking away from the deal, can be

viewed as a high-risk move, and you certainly don't want to enter into it too easily. It is a strategy to use with a customer who has negotiated every point to death, who simply will not move toward an agreement, or will not be reasonable. An unreasonable customer is one who agrees to the benefits, cannot defend his or her objection, but continues to repeat it; agrees to *cost/benefits*, and to superiority of total offer, but continues to reject your terms without justification. It is a strategy to use when you have *exhausted* every alternative and idea, and the customer is behaving irrationally. It should be used with customers with whom, after *extensive dialogue*, testing for agreement and understanding, resolving objections, and total offer analysis and summarizing, a WIN–WIN does not seem possible. *The exit close should be used as a way to avoid being the LOSE side of an inevitable WIN–LOSE.* Then you should use the exit close.

To close, you might say, "We have been working on this for X time. We agree on A, B and C, but cannot resolve D. It seems we are at an impasse. Perhaps at this time we should conclude, since it does not look as if this can be resolved."

Say this as you make definite closing gestures. Put your pen away, and gather your papers. Remain *silent* and wait for the customer to reply. After the exit close statement, three outcomes are possible:

- The customer will agree with your analysis and the negotiation will come to an end (perhaps to be reopened later).
- The customer will shake hands on the deal there and then or very soon thereafter.
- The customer will tell you what is really going on.

Another, possibly less drastic, version of the exit

close is, "We have been talking about . . . for . . . . I think it's time you talk to other bankers. As soon as you test this for yourself, we can talk again."

When you initiate the exit close you must be *prepared to walk away* from the deal. In any negotiation it is important to care about closing the deal, but not to care *so much* that your desire for the deal interferes with your ability to negotiate a WIN–WIN.

The high-risk is that the exit close can lead to a final closing down in the negotiation. You must be able to accept this risk. If the negotiation does shut down not to be reopened, you will have saved valuable time and avoided a bad deal/agreement. If it does reopen, you may be able to reopen on a new footing. In any case, you will not be involved in a bad deal.

One successful exit close was used by a banker who finally tested a large corporate customer. This customer had been totally unreasonable. He delayed making decisions for a three-month period, continued to get concession after concession from the banker at each meeting, and approached every subsequent meeting as if it were the starting point to begin negotiating for more concessions. Finally the banker, after attending the negotiation seminar, decided that she would use the exit close if the situation were not resolved at the next meeting. She used the exit close on a Friday, and on the following Monday morning the customer called her to accept her deal! Not all situations will end as positively, but at the very least you can avoid wasting your time and squandering your resources on WIN–LOSE deals.

Again, as you employ the exit close, be sure to leave the door open for future deals. For moments when it may be tempting to storm out and burn a bridge, you can learn a lesson from the misfortunes that befell the great Odysseus.

As the story is told, Odysseus blinded the one-eyed giant Polyphemus, son of Poseidon, the God of the Sea. Odysseus and his men were trapped in the giant's cave but they managed to escape by tying themselves to the bellies of the sheep that were going out to pasture. When Odysseus and his sailors reached their ship, Odysseus could not control his desire to shout at and taunt the now-blind Polyphemus. In anger, Polyphemus threw a boulder which almost sank Odysseus' ship. The sailors pleaded with Odysseus to stop tormenting the giant, but Odysseus would not listen to them. He went further and to make sure Polyphemus *knew who hurt him*, he identified himself as Odysseus. In doing so he overlooked an essential characteristic of human nature: revenge. With the knowledge of who caused his blindness, Polyphemus enlisted the help of his father, who punished Odysseus by delaying his return home for 10 years. Odysseus, one of the greatest negotiators, paid dearly for this ego satisfaction.

As mentioned previously, some negotiators go so far as not to smile *too* enthusiastically at the end of a WIN—WIN negotiation. They keep their egos under wraps.

USING THE NEGOTIATION ENVIRONMENT

The Setting

The environment in which a negotiation takes place has an impact on its outcome. Where parties sit, where the negotiation is held, decor, and lighting can influence how the negotiation proceeds. Rectangular tables tend to reinforce adversarial positions by setting up "us" against "them" configuration. 'Us" against "them" also blocks eye contact. Round tables encourage good eye contact, focus discussions, and foster a collaborative approach. Even the comfort and stability of chairs can have an impact. Arm rests, steady bases, and up-right backs are most conducive to effective negotiation. Lighting should be comfortable, neither glaring nor dim.

Whether at your own office or your customer's, you should try to arrange right-angle (consultative) seating rather than lock-horns (adversarial) seating. Of course, for a consultative negotiation, a desk is the least preferred arrangement, since it sets up a barrier between the negotiators. Although it can be advantageous for you to be on your own turf (or on neutral ground), you should gracefully accept an invitation to the customer's facility. While you can have more control in your own environment, you can also learn a good deal about your customer by observing his or her environment and seeing him or her in it.

The important point about environment is that it can be controlled. You should avoid negotiating in a totally unfamiliar environment even if it means stopping by for X reason beforehand or arriving a bit early. By "creating" the negotiation site—that is, rearranging seating, lighting, and so on—you can create a positive environment in which you can maintain control. By being aware of the importance of the environment, you can avoid being a victim of environmental tactics, such as glaring sun or a lower chair, when they are clearly being used to manipulate you. Simply request that they be changed. Say, "The sun is too glaring. Can we change rooms or adjust . . . ?"

In short, the negotiation environment can work against you or for you. It's up to you.

Special Negotiation Situations

RENEGOTIATION

Eventually the time comes when you must renegotiate a price or terms that you and your customer have agreed upon. Whether you have good news or bad news to impart, do so immediately.

When it is *time to renegotiate* a loan, for example, with good news for the customer because you recognize that the present rate/fee is too high and you are prepared to lower it, *you should be the one to initiate the reduction* with the customer. If a competitor is the one to point out an inappropriately high rate/fee to the customer, you are apt to find yourself in a price war. In price wars, if you preserve the deal, you will usually end up with a lower rate/fee than if you initially brought it to the customer's attention and negotiated a fair price. You can use renegotiation to meet with the customer and strengthen the relationship, often getting more business.

For example, as a result of a merger, two customers became eligible for a volume discount for a service they both received from the same bank. The bank failed to bring this to the customer's attention. When the new treasurer learned about this, he took the opportunity to "make his mark" by changing institutions.

The same principle applies when a deal is being renegotiated because of bad news for the customer. For example, if you must increase the customer's rate or move the customer from an unsecured to a secured basis, or if you must now charge a fee for a service the customer previously got for "free," because balances no longer exist or new modules have been added on, don't procrastinate. Break the news yourself; you can invite a senior manager to join you but do not delegate it upstairs or downstairs. Carefully and patiently *explain* the *differences* in the new and old deal or situation and your *reasons* for the new terms, since the customer will need this information for his or her own knowledge and for explanation to management. Get agreement on the difference and demonstrate how the new deal will satisfy the customer's current *needs*. Some customers may lack sophistication about cost, profitability, or bank requirements. Use this as an opportunity to take a more consultative role. This is especially true when a customer is taken aback by or is resistant to the new requests ("The bank never needed this before!").

DECLINING

Even in this competitive environment, declining deals is necessary either because the agreement would be a LOSE for the bank or it is not appropriate business for the institution. Negotiating your way out of a deal without causing hard feelings, especially after you have shown interest in the deal or initiated it, can be the ultimate negotiating challenge. Exiting from a long-standing relationship can be even more traumatic.

Once again, it is very important that you avoid burning bridges here, and that you do whatever possible to support the relationship so that minimal, if any, damage is done. By remaining consultative and empathetic and presenting your "business reasons," you can usually satisfy the client emotionally if not financially.

Point out to the customer how he or she can benefit. You can say, "We have a high regard for your company, but are you sure you need three banks . . . ? We have tried repeatedly over the past few years to expand the range of services to you . . . . The pricing we require is higher than your lead bank's because . . . ." If you can't participate in the deal or you cannot continue the relationship, you should be prepared to explain why. Focus on business reasons and be very clear to the customer that the decision is not a personal one.

When your customer is offered a *low rate* that you consider to be a fool's bid from a competitor trying to "buy" the business, a bid that you absolutely cannot profitably match, under most circumstances do not agree to match it or you will hurt your profitability and credibility. In most situations say that you cannot match the price and then tell the customer why, pointing out what he or she may be risking for what may be a temporary gain. One banker said, "I want this deal. I know we can do a great job for you. I also have confidence in my pricing and know that long-term relationships are built on WIN–WIN. My question to you without attacking X (the competitor) is, 'How long will they stick with you?' All banks are looking at profitability and cutting back." Another banker pointed to his track record with private placements and preserved his price and relationship because he demonstrated value added.

Do not accept WIN–LOSE deals since they usually do not lead to good relationships. This was obvious in the situation in which a good customer came to his bank with a fool's bid from a competitor bank. His present banker knew that the deal offered by the competitor would be a bad deal for the newcomer bank (WIN–LOSE). Rather than decline the deal, however, he *finally* agreed to match it. In spite of this concession, the customer chose to go with the new bank! Why? First, he resented all of his bank's delays, and second, since his bank did finally concede he questioned the fairness of his bank's original deal. Within a few months, the new bank found that it could not live with the terms of the agreement and tried to impose numerous restrictions after the fact. This damaged the relationship between the customer and his new bank. The customer reestablished his relationship with his original bank, but now negotiates harder than before because the bank folded once!

When you decline, even if you think the bank should have participated in the deal or made the concession, you must present a unified front and avoid the temptation to side with the customer. Instead you can say, "I really went to bat for you, but at this time we cannot ... because ..." (explain why). Do not say, "I think my management is wrong but it is out of my hands."

On some occasions, regardless of how well you negotiated to satisfy the needs of both sides and regardless of how excellent your package was, the customer may decline to do the transaction with you and opt to go with a competitor. In this situation you should:

- Find out why the customer is going with the competition ("To help me understand, can you tell me, what led to this decision . . . ?")
- Check if the deal is signed—again, it ain't over 'til it's over!
- State your genuine disappointment in not getting the deal.
- Thank the customer for consideration of your proposal.
- Express interest in the "next deal"—ask what else is on their plate *now*—or if not appropriate, ask them in the next week.
- Check back with key customers to find out how things worked out—you still may get that deal!
- *Spare that bridge!*

You should be as professional when you exit from a deal as when you shake hands on one.

TELEPHONE NEGOTIATIONS

Negotiating on the telephone is a necessity, but it can be fraught with problems. The telephone is *not* the best tool for negotiating. There is no face-to-face contact and, therefore, no opportunity to read body language and other nonverbal gestures. It is easier for customers to say "No" over the telephone than in person. The distance created by the telephone can distort things, making it easier to minimize the importance of a "small point" that is not small. The natural tendency to rush on the telephone also leads to mistakes. If you keep these danger areas in mind, however, you can use the telephone to maintain a dialogue and close a deal.

The following guidelines will help you offset the disadvantages of negotiating on the telephone:

- Be the one to make the call—*or return* it if you are not *fully prepared.* Preparation and control can go hand in hand.
- Make a *checklist* of all topics to be covered *before* making the call and use it as an agenda to cover topics. This will help avoid the omissions that are all too common in telephone negotiations.
- Take detailed *notes* and keep a record of the conversation since customers will take notes and read them back to you at appropriate times, such as "On March 10, you said you had no problem with . . . ."
- Do not interrupt.
- Be the one to confirm quickly in writing.
- Become comfortable with the "squawk box," conference call, and speaker phones. Ask who is in the room or on the line.
- Watch out for the "small point." Recognize that using the telephone may lead you to minimize the importance of the subject under discussion. Customers can use the telephone to get you to make easy concessions if you are not alert and cautious.
- Never give a quick answer, especially a firm "Yes" or "No" by telephone unless you have no doubt about your position. Telephones seem to force closure by the end of the call, so *be careful.*
- Avoid interruptions during the call. Concentrate.
- Use a calculator and double-check everything, since errors by telephone are common.
- Be selective about the issues you choose to discuss, and when possible avoid complex issues.
- If you find yourself negotiating over the telephone

with a new party who is substituting for your original contact, be sure to establish rapport. Remember to make a new introduction, *define roles*. Find out who this person is. Review the status of negotiation so far, ask him or her for feedback, and so on.

- During a conference call with your analyst, colleague, or manager, arrange the seating, if possible, so that members of your team can *see* one another and write/pass notes to one another. Use the hold button to break for discussions.
- Don't use the telephone if you can't afford to be told "No." Arrange a face-to-face meeting if a negative outcome would be a real problem for you.
- Expect rude behavior or unreasonable demands that the other party would not be likely to make in person.

TEAM NEGOTIATIONS

There are many reasons to use teams during a negotiation. Two (or more) heads are usually better than one, or specialized expertise may be needed. Also, customers frequently negotiate in teams, for example, with lawyers, and so on, since it is usually easy for them to produce a team. Negotiating in a team can help you balance the numbers and equalize the power.

Team negotiations call for special preparation. The word *team* indicates the critical need for planning and tight coordination prior to and during the negotiation.

In preparing for team negotiations, the leader should help the team:

- Establish and agree upon objectives.

- Define roles (lead, team players, expert, concessions tracker, etc.) so that team members can prepare for and fulfill their roles in a supportive and effective manner.

During the team negotiation, whatever role you play, you should:

- Always support your teammate. Do not *contradict* your colleague/s—"a house divided . . . ." Don't play an obvious "good guy, bad guy."
- Recognize "good guy/bad guy" from the other team. If they begin to overdo it, say, "Perhaps we should break while you discuss your position."
- Remain active even if your colleague is doing most of the negotiating (so much is happening—two heads are better than one) and show support in your comments, nonverbal signals such as nodding in agreement, and so on. Concentrate.
- Take notes.
- Keep eye contact.
- Arrange seating so that you can "read" your teammates' signals (and discreetly signal them). Also, sit with your group, not off to the side or out of easy contact, during the negotiation.
- Give support or line comments to your team members whenever appropriate.
- Arrange seating so that there are *no empty seats* between participants.
- Do not go in different directions out of fear. Demonstrate unity and confidence (even in the face of loss). Mask feelings of fear.
- Ask for *time-out* if you have a new idea or a position that contradicts your team member's position—"Something has occurred to me that we haven't talked about, may we confer (step out)" or

ask for a break by saying, "We've been meeting . . . . I'd like to call my office."

- Remember that you do not have "telepathy" with your team members. Communicate with and observe one another.
- Listen for *key* lines/ideas from your team members, particularly from your leader. For example, recognize when the lead negotiator has *closed* with a comment such as, "Joe and I have spent a lot of time and we think that this can work." Recognize this as a closing cue and maintain silence. *Do not reopen* by saying, "We also thought of . . . ."
- Remember you are a team.
- Remember it's okay if your manager gets most of the attention during a specific negotiation.
- Do not allow side conversations to take place haphazardly. The leader should always be aware of what is going on and side conversations of any consequence must be orchestrated and planned.
- Never reach an agreement without consulting with your team unless it is *exactly* what you know the team would want and you wish to seize the moment.

The following example will serve to demonstrate how important it is to negotiate as a solid team. A team of two bankers was negotiating with two customers. The four were hammering out price in a consultative way. The price was already in the customer's acceptable range. Then a side conversation about a detail developed between the less senior customer and the less senior, nuts-and-bolts banker. Thanks to this side conversation, the senior customer *seized the moment*. He said to his banker peer, "If you give us . . . , we'll take those terms. Can you do that?'' The banker, bereft of his nuts-and-bolts role player, said, ''Yes.'' The customer said, ''Do we have a deal?'' and put out his hand. They shook hands. Needless to say, the revised terms favored the customer. What the banker should have done was said, ''This sounds very interesting. Let me pass this by my colleague.'' The point is, if you have a team, use it!

CONCLUSION

The introduction to this book defines a successful financial sales negotiation as ''reaching agreement on a change in price or terms between what the customer needs and what you need.'' In today's highly volatile and competitive financial sales environment, such changes are no longer blocks to opportunity—they *are* your opportunity.

Today's financial services customer can choose from so many alternatives that the traditional long-term relationship between the customer and the financial sales institution that serves his or her needs would seem threatened with extinction. Indeed it is, but not because of these growing customer choices. Rather, the greatest peril posed to the customer/institution bond is a banker's inability to understand his or her customer's needs and satisfy those needs while at the same time creating and sustaining profitable relationships in the face of such change.

True, the risks agile competitors pose to the once stable customer/institution relationship are expanding, while the profit margins available to fuel it are shrinking. But like the human species and unlike the dinosaurs, today's successful financial sales professional can *adapt* to such changes, converting them to relationship and transactional gain. By practicing the strategies and tactics of consultative negotiation outlined in this book, you can learn to protect ongoing profitable relationships and develop new ones.

It all starts with you. While reading this book, many of you have undoubtedly experienced *déjà vu*, seeing the same negotiation principles reappear in different negotiating situations. This is how it should be, for negotiation is a matter of nuance. It requires mastery of the same hard lessons again and again, both within single transactions and over several.

Perhaps your most intense flashbacks came from your personal negotiating history: the great deals that you shaped, the precarious deals that you saved by using instinctive WIN–WIN tactics, as well as the WIN–LOSE deals you are living or dying with today because you could not recognize and control—or walk away from—an adversarial.

This book was written to help you become your own negotiation coach—at your desk while preparing or at the negotiation table working through a deal. The message to yourself is clear: WIN–WIN or WALK.

CONSULTATIVE NEGOTIATION CHECKLIST

Everyone likes checklists. The best ones are the ones you keep in your head. Next best are the ones you can carry with you for quick reference. The following checklist is offered for just that purpose.

- **Prepare**
  Use lead time to identify needs on *all* sides.
  Aim/keep aspirations high.
  Set objectives—identify essentials and trade-offs.
- **Open/counteropen**
  Establish rapport.
  Summarize and check.
  Confidently present terms.
- **Convert demands to needs—Ask questions throughout the negotiation**
  Why won't you give guarantees?
  What are you *comparing* this to in thinking it is too expensive?
  How did you arrive at that figure?
  What is your *concern* with . . . ?
- **Recognize/control adversarial tactics**
  Extreme position.
  Threats.
  No information and no concessions.
- **Trade bargain**—Give nothing away
  Trade for value
  Trade slowly—one at a time for equal value.
  Keep total package in mind—get *full* shopping list before trading.
  Take notes/listen.
- **Preserve price/terms/total yield**
  Be confident—sit up, speak up.

Be silent after stating price.
Connect price and value.
- **Close**
Summarize/act.
Never burn a bridge.
Remember satisfying dollar needs only will not
satisfy the customer.
WIN–WIN, or WALK.

For a wallet-sized checklist please send a self-address-
ed envelope to:

> Linda Richardson
> 1608 Walnut St.
> Suite 402
> Philadelphia, PA 19103

INDEX

145